Publication Number 30

Duke University Commonwealth-Studies Center

*The International Law of
the Great Lakes*

Duke University Commonwealth-Studies Center Publications

1. *The British Commonwealth,* by Frank H. Underhill   2. *South Africa,* by Hector Menteith Robertson   3. *Some Comparative Aspects of Irish Law,* by Alfred Gaston Donaldson   4. *Economic Analysis and Policy in Underdeveloped Countries,* by P. T. Bauer   5. *The Higher Public Service of the Commonwealth of Australia,* by Howard A. Scarrow   6. *Economic Opinion and Policy in Ceylon,* by Henry M. Oliver, Jr.   7. *Problems of the New Commonwealth,* by Sir Ivor Jennings   8. *Commonwealth Perspectives,* by Nicholas Mansergh *et al.*   9. *Evolving Canadian Federalism,* by A. R. M. Lower, F. R. Scott *et al.*   10. *The Commonwealth Economy in Southeast Asia,* by T. H. Silcock   11. *Public Expenditures in Australia,* by B. U. Ratchford   12. *The American Economic Impact on Canada,* by Hugh G. J. Aitken, John J. Deutsch, W. A. Mackintosh *et al.*   13. *Tradition, Values, and Socio-Economic Development,* edited by Ralph Braibanti and Joseph J. Spengler   14. *The Growth of Canadian Policies in External Affairs,* by Hugh L. Keenleyside *et al.*   15. *Canadian Economic Thought,* by Craufurd D. W. Goodwin   16. *Economic Systems of the Commonwealth,* edited by Calvin B. Hoover   17. *The Nigerian Political Scene,* edited by Robert O. Tilman and Taylor Cole   18. *Administration and Economic Development in India,* edited by Ralph Braibanti and Joseph J. Spengler   19. *Canada–United States Treaty Relations,* edited by David R. Deener   20. *Postprimary Education and Political and Economic Development,* edited by Don C. Piper and Taylor Cole   21. *Bureaucratic Transition in Malaya,* by Robert O. Tilman   22. *The West African Commonwealth,* by C. W. Newbury   23. *The Transfer of Institutions,* edited by William B. Hamilton   24. *Economic Enquiry in Australia,* by Craufurd D. W. Goodwin   25. *A Decade of the Commonwealth, 1955–1964,* edited by W. B. Hamilton, Kenneth Robinson, and C. D. W. Goodwin   26. *Research on the Bureaucracy of Pakistan,** by Ralph Braibanti   27. *The International Law Standard and Commonwealth Developments,* by Robert R. Wilson *et al.*   28. *Asian Bureaucratic Systems Emergent from the British Imperial Tradition,* by Ralph Braibanti and asssociates   29. *Canada and "Imperial Defense,"* by Richard A. Preston

* Program in Comparative Studies on Southern Asia publication.

The International Law of the Great Lakes

A Study of Canadian–United States Co-operation

Don Courtney Piper

Published for the
Duke University Commonwealth-Studies Center
Duke University Press, Durham, N. C.
1967

Printed in the United States of America
by Kingsport Press, Inc., Kingsport, Tenn.

To my family—each one is a part of this effort.

Foreword

International legal relations of Canada with the United States have involved a variety of questions concerning the Great Lakes. Among these are, necessarily, matters relating to public international law. In the present study Professor Piper, with characteristic industry, thorough documentation, and careful weighing of the evidence, has illumined means utilized in effort to solve legal problems that have developed. From the time when the United States unsuccessfully invoked natural law (in support of its claimed right to navigate the Canadian section of the St. Lawrence) to the present time (when there is apparently no longer appeal to such a concept as the Harmon Doctrine as a proper statement of a general principle of law) there has been, the author finds, a proclivity on the part of the two neighbors to depend chiefly upon diplomacy or *ad hoc* arrangements.

Jurisdiction over vessels, enforcement of criminal law, regulation of fisheries, pilotage, the use of canals, diversion of waters, and adjustments to the interests of third states (as under most-favored-nation commitments) have figured in relations between Canada and the United States. The author notes that the Boundary Waters Convention of 1909 has replaced some earlier treaty arrangements, but he points out that some lacunae still remain. He observes that it is time for the parties to make the navigation of the entire Great Lakes system (including Lake Michigan) a matter of "permanent right." It is reasonable to envisage a continuing regard for public international law in this as in other areas of relationship which Canada has had with the United States.

Following completion of his graduate education the author was a research associate and subsequently, for two years, Executive

Foreword

Secretary of the Commonwealth-Studies Center at Duke University. He was also a member of the Duke Department of Political Science. He has participated in various study conferences relating to the Commonwealth, including one held in 1964 at the Villa Serbelloni, Bellagio, Italy (jointly arranged by the Institute of Commonwealth Studies at the University of London and the Duke University Commonwealth-Studies Center). Since 1964 he has been a member of the Department of Government and Politics at the University of Maryland.

Publication of the present volume in the Duke University Commonwealth-Studies Series was made possible by grants from the Carnegie Corporation. For opinions expressed or conclusions reached, however, the author alone is responsible.

Students of history, politics, economics, public law and of broader aspects of international relations should find in the present concise study a highly useful record of inter-governmental effort. Professor Piper finds that, in general, despite some frustrations, this effort has been successful, and that the party states have moved toward a sense of community in the sharing of their common heritage.

ROBERT R. WILSON

Preface

This study, an attempt to extract from the conventional rules and customary principles of international law that govern Canadian-American relations those rules, principles, and practices that are applicable specifically to the Great Lakes, is one of narrow scope. Because of its limited scope, many other important legal problems that have arisen between the two countries have of necessity been excluded. It is suggested, however, that the body of international law that pertains to the Great Lakes is considerable and impressive.

The political scientist interested in international law has as his task the study of the legal principles which govern the relations between nations—in this instance the legal principles which govern Canadian-American relations relative to the lakes. In making the study, I have oftentimes relied heavily on the works of diplomatic historians; however, I have tried to keep foremost in mind the realization that the task here is to present the legal principles at issue and not to provide merely another history of the negotiations and developments. Consequently, I have endeavored not to allow the analysis to become embedded in historical detail but to cut through the detail and expose the rules of law that are present. For this reason the analysis is perhaps more precise, more specific, and, in some matters, shorter than would be expected of the diplomatic historian or the student of international relations. As a foundation for the legal analysis, the international political factors that provide the environment for the legal regime are discussed. Moreover, the legal problems of the St. Lawrence Seaway have been included only insofar as they affect the Great Lakes specifically.

The emphasis is on the public international law (i.e., the law between states); consequently some municipal laws that pertain to the lakes as a purely domestic matter have not been examined. Certain municipal laws that pertain both to the high seas and to the lakes have been discussed to the extent necessary to illustrate their general scope and application to the Great Lakes.

The greater portion of the material utilized in this study is in published form. In addition I have used the Department of State file for the period 1906–1941 in the National Archives and the Governor General file and the Robert Borden, George Gibbons, and Wilfrid Laurier papers in the Public Archives of Canada.

In its original form, this study was a doctoral dissertation submitted to the Department of Political Science at Duke University. It has undergone several years of additional research, reflection, and writing. I am indebted to the Department of Political Science of Duke University for financial assistance that enabled me to undertake research for a summer in Washington, D.C., Ottawa, and Toronto. In addition the General Research Board of the University of Maryland provided grants that enabled me to complete the final preparation of the manuscript and to have it typed. This assistance is gratefully acknowledged.

Many have assisted me with their ideas, guidance, encouragement, and insight over the past several years. I am indebted to all of them for this assistance. I am responsible for any shortcomings or failings.

The man who has had the greatest impact on this study is Robert R. Wilson, James B. Duke Professor of Political Science, Duke University. From his initial suggestion of the topic, he has been a continual source of refreshing encouragement and perceptive guidance. I have had the benefit and satisfaction of this encouragement and guidance for more than seven years—first as a student and then as a junior colleague. No one has begun an academic career under more favorable and pleasant circumstances.

D.C.P.

College Park, Maryland
November, 1966

Contents

List of Abbreviations

AJIL	*American Journal of International Law*
Am. Jur.	*American Jurisprudence*
BYIL	*British Yearbook of International Law*
C.F.R.	*Code of Federal Regulations* (1958 edition)
C.J.S.	*Corpus Juris Secundum*
D.L.R.	*Dominion Law Reports* (Canada)
Ex. C.R.	*Reports of the Exchequer Court of Canada*
F.	*Federal Reporter* (U. S. Courts of Appeal, 1880–1924)
F. 2d	*Federal Reporter* (U. S. Courts of Appeal, 1924—)
F. Supp.	*Federal Supplement* (U. S. District Courts and Court of Claims)
Fed. Cas.	*Federal Cases* (U. S. Courts of Appeal, 1789–1897)
For. Rel.	*Papers Relating to the Foreign Relations of the United States*
Hackworth, *Digest.*	Green H. Hackworth, *Digest of International Law.* 8 vols. Washington: Government Printing Office, 1940–1944
How.	Howard, *U. S. Supreme Court Reports,* 1843–1860
Hyde, *International Law.*	Charles Cheney Hyde, *International Law Chiefly as Interpreted and Applied by the United States.* 3 vols. 2d ed. revised. Boston: Little, Brown Co., 1945.
L.N.T.S.	League of Nations Treaty Series.
Lauterpacht, *Oppenheim's International Law.*	L. Oppenheim, *International Law, a Treatise.* 7th ed. Edited by H. Lauterpacht. London: Longmans, 1948. Vol. I.
M.P.R.	*Maritime Provinces Reports* (Canada)

Mich.	*Michigan Reports*
Moore, *Digest.*	John Bassett Moore, *A Digest of International Law.* 8 vols. Washington: Government Printing Office, 1906
N.E.	*Northeastern Reporter* (United States)
N.W.	*Northwestern Reporter* (United States)
Ont.L.R.	*Ontario Law Reports*
Ont.W.R.	*Ontario Weekly Reporter*
Ops. Atty. Gen.	*Official Opinions of the Attorneys General of the United States*
Pr. R.	*Reports of the Cases Determined in the Practice Court and Chambers* (Canada)
Que. K.B.	*Quebec Official Reports, King's Bench*
Rev. Stat.	*The Revised Statutes of Canada*
S.C.R.	*Reports of the Supreme Court of Canada*
SOR, Consolidation.	Canada, *Statutory Orders and Regulations, Consolidation* (1955 edition)
Stat.	United States, *Statutes at Large*
T.I.A.S.	Treaties and Other International Acts Series (United States)
U.C.C.P.	*Upper Canada Common Pleas*
U. S.	*United States Reports* (Supreme Court)
U.S.C.	*United States Code* (1958 edition and Supplements)
U.S.T.	*United States Treaties and Other International Agreements*
W.W.R.	*Western Weekly Reports* (Canada)
Wall.	Wallace, *U. S. Supreme Court Reports, 1863–1874*
Wheat.	Wheaton, *U. S. Supreme Court Reports, 1816–1827*
Whiteman, *Digest*	Marjorie M. Whiteman, *Digest of International Law.* Washington: Government Printing Office, 1963—

*The International Law of
the Great Lakes*

· 1 ·

The Environment of the International
Legal Regime

If public international law is defined as "the standard of conduct, at a given time, for states and other entities subject
thereto,"[1] it would appear logical that the more extensive the
relations between two states the more comprehensive are the
conventional and customary rules and principles of international
law that govern their relations. This is certainly true with regard
to Canada and the United States. As contiguous countries whose
common frontier runs more than three thousand miles, and as
sharers of a common cultural and political heritage, the American
community and the Canadian community have naturally encountered the need of public law, along with other means, for regulating their shared interests.

As of 1965 there were in force nearly two hundred bilateral
treaties and agreements governing the relations between the two
North American neighbors.[2] These treaties and agreements encompass more than thirty different topics, and comprise such
matters as atomic energy, boundaries, consuls, economic co-operation, extradition, finance, fisheries, health and sanitation, high-
ways, labor, maritime and navigation matters, patents, military
forces, pacific settlement of disputes, property, smuggling, taxation, telecommunications, trade and commerce, and weather sta-
tions.[3] In addition to this comprehensive conventional law in

1. Whiteman, *Digest*, I, 1.
2. U. S. Department of State, *Treaties in Force: A List of Treaties and Other
International Agreements of the United States in Force on January 1, 1965*
(Department of State Publication 7817, 1965), pp. 23–33.
3. For an insightful discussion of United States-Canadian treaties, see David R.
Deener, ed., *Canada—United States Treaty Relations* (Durham, N. C.: Duke
University Press, 1963).

force between the two countries, the principles of customary international law on such matters as the privileges and immunities of diplomatic representatives, the minimum standard for the treatment of aliens, the nature and extent of territorial jurisdiction, and the rights and immunities of sovereign states before foreign tribunals are also applicable.

Relations between Canada and the United States have also involved the occasional resort to the procedures recognized by international law, noticeably to the mode of international arbitration, with the resultant enunciation of some principles of adjective law, such as that for settlement of international disputes. Such disputes as those involving the Alaskan boundary, the North Atlantic fisheries, the Bering Sea fur seals, the smelter at Trail, British Columbia, the *I'm Alone,* the *Tattler,* the *Jessie, Thomas F. Bayard,* and the *Peschawha,* and the Cayuga Indians, have been peacefully resolved by resort to international arbitration and the resulting interpretation and application of international law. The history of the peaceful settlement of Canadian-American disputes has led one writer to characterize it as "a treasury of precious experience in the solution of international disputes."[4]

This brief illustrative statement suggests that there has been extensive experience in the use and application of the principles of international law in Canadian-American relations. Resort to law has served the interests of both countries. The purpose here is to consider the substance and application of the rules of international law pertinent to Canadian-American relations with regard to the Great Lakes (i.e., the rules and principles of action which are binding between Canada and the United States in their relations with one another in matters pertaining to the Great Lakes and their connecting and tributary waters). The body of rules involves not only conventional law specifically applicable to the Great Lakes, but also certain general principles of the law of nations that have been modified to meet the lake conditions. The investigation necessarily involves the examination of some reciprocal municipal legislation applicable to lake situations, and deci-

4. P. E. Corbett, *The Settlement of Canadian-American Disputes* (New Haven: Yale University Press, 1937), p. 2.

sions of municipal courts and of international arbitral tribunals.

At the outset it may appear to be something of an anomaly to speak of applying principles and procedures of international law to the Great Lakes since they are not international waters but are part of the national territories of Canada and the United States. The physical and economic facts of the Great Lakes illustrate, however, the need for the application of the rules and principles of international law. The lakes are the largest such body of water in the world as well as the largest body of fresh water in the world. Their total area comprises more than ninety-five thousand square miles, of which approximately two-thirds is within American jurisdiction and one-third within Canadian jurisdiction. The Great Lakes drainage basin totals more than 291,680 square miles. Since the opening of the St. Lawrence Seaway, there has been a continuous waterway of 2,347 miles into the heart of the North American continent with a channel of sufficient depth to permit navigation by ocean-going vessels. Water diverted from the American side of the Niagara and St. Lawrence rivers produces more than fifty million dollars worth of hydroelectric power annually, with an equal, if not greater, amount of power being generated on the Canadian side. Two-thirds of the Canadian population is located within the Great Lakes basin; on the opposite side such populous American cities as Chicago, Cleveland, Detroit, Milwaukee, and Buffalo dot the shoreline.

Given this situation, it is difficult to envisage the extensive development of the Great Lakes without the beneficial application of the rules and principles of international law. Since every state has exclusive jurisdiction over the territory within its boundaries, the resources of the Great Lakes could have been independently developed in each country as a purely internal matter without any consideration given to the rights or interests of the other riparian state or without any reciprocal extension of rights to the citizens of the other state. Such an occurrence would certainly have frustrated the full development and optimum utilization of the resources of the Great Lakes. Fortunately, this was not done. Since the earliest days of American independence, there has been a mutual awareness of the interests of the other state and a realization that the full potential of the lakes' resources could be developed only by the utilization of applicable customary rules of international law and the formulation of special conventional rules.

Before we begin the specific study of the international legal regime for the Great Lakes, we need to make some general observations relative to some historical landmarks in the development of that regime. It should be remembered that it was not until 1923 that Canada obtained full powers in treaty-making. Until that time treaties were concluded by the United Kingdom on behalf of the Dominion. Accordingly, many of the conventional rules relative to the Great Lakes and Canadian—United States relations in general were concluded with the United Kingdom and have devolved upon Canada following its attainment of full political independence.[5] Throughout the nineteenth century the United States apparently took the position that since Canada did not enjoy full independence, the United States authorities could not have any direct diplomatic relations with Canadian representatives. In this regard it is instructive to mention a minor incident that occurred in 1895 regarding the formulation of common rules of the road to govern navigation on the Great Lakes. When differences arose over the substance of the rules, the British Ambassador suggested the advisability of "direct intercommunication between the United States Government and the Canadian government." Secretary of State Olney replied that he was unable to regard the suggestion "as seriously proposing that the Government of the United States shall enter into diplomatic negotiations with the Dominion of Canada upon the subject referred to." He was willing, however, to appoint experts to investigate the matter and pave the way for negotiations through regular channels.[6]

Although the 1909 Boundary Waters Treaty was concluded with the United Kingdom and signed by the British Ambassador,

5. It is instructive to note that Art. XXVI of the Treaty of Washington (1871) that relates to the free use of the St. Lawrence River is listed in *Treaties in Force* as being in force with the United Kingdom and not with Canada. The provision, of course, is presently relative to Canada.
6. *For. Rel.* (1895), I, 714–719.

it played an important role in the development of Canada's independent international status. The treaty was negotiated by a Canadian, George Gibbons. Moreover, Canada enjoyed an equal status with the United States on the International Joint Commission that was established by the treaty and in the settlement of boundary waters problems.[7] To Gibbons and other Canadians the prospect of dealing directly with the United States was welcome because it was believed that the United States would no longer bully Canada once the British were out of the way.[8]

As a matter of historical interest the Great Lakes is also well known as the site of the *Caroline* affair, which occurred in December, 1837. It involved the burning on the American side of the Niagara River by Canadian soldiers of an American vessel suspected of carrying supplies to the Canadian rebels. Before the incident was ultimately resolved, there occurred numerous exchanges between British and United States authorities concerning the obligations of neutrals under international law, the justification for actions in self-defense, and the individual responsibility for acts of state.[9]

7. See Edgar W. McInnis, *The Unguarded Frontier* (New York: Doubleday, Doran, 1942), p. 320; and Oscar Douglas Skelton, *Life and Letters of Sir Wilfrid Laurier* (New York: Century, 1922), II, 363.

8. See letters of Gibbons to Laurier, Gibbons Papers, Vol. 8, nos. 222, 477 (Public Archives of Canada). At the time Sir Wilfrid Laurier was the Canadian Prime Minister.

9. For the correspondence of this affair, see William R. Manning, *Diplomatic Correspondence of the United States: Canadian Relations: 1784–1860* (Washington: Carnegie Endowment for International Peace, 1943), III, 45–51 ff.

2

Definition and Delineation of the International Boundary

One of the fundamental problems that confronted the American and British Commissioners at Paris in 1782 was the establishment of a satisfactory international boundary between the newly independent United States and the British possessions to the north.[1] Although the Commissioners considered a number of proposals,[2] they realized that the Great Lakes was a natural boundary and stipulated in the treaty of peace that part of the northern boundary of the United States would be the "middle" of Lakes Ontario, Erie, Huron, and Superior, and their connecting water communications.[3] Although there have been some minor adjust-

1. For a brief discussion of the major and minor boundary disputes between the United States and Canada, see Hugh L. Keenleyside and G. S. Brown, *Canada and the United States* (rev. ed.; New York: Knopf, 1952), pp. 137–210.
2. The original instructions prepared by Congress in 1779 for the American Commissioners called for a northern boundary along the Nipissing line, i.e., a line commencing at the junction of the Connecticut River and the 45th Parallel, along that parallel to the St. Lawrence River and thence to the south end of Lake Nipissing. Another proposal called for the boundary along the 45th Parallel until it intersected the Mississippi River. The British selected the middle line boundary over the latter proposal. For the text of the Commissioners' instructions, see Francis Wharton, ed., *The Revolutionary Diplomatic Correspondence of the United States* (Washington: Government Printing Office, 1889), III, 293. For a map illustrating the Nipissing line and the other proposed boundary lines, see Samuel Flagg Bemis, *The Diplomacy of the American Revolution* (New York: D. Appleton-Century, 1935), p. 228. See also *ibid.*, p. 238; and Wharton, *op. cit.*, V, 845, 851, 856.
3. Art. II. A careful reading of this article will reveal one variance in the repetition of the language describing the boundary line through each lake and water communication between the lakes. The description of the boundary from Lake Huron to Lake Superior provides that the line shall go to the water communication between the two lakes "thence through Lake Superior." In this instance there is no description of the boundary through the water communication between the two lakes, as in all other cases. When this was pointed out during the settlement of the boundary under Article VII of the Treaty of Ghent, the Commissioners treated the omission as a mistake and proceeded on the assumption that the treaty-makers intended for the boundary to pass through the water communication between the two lakes. See John Bassett Moore, *History and*

ments in the boundary, the present international boundary through the Great Lakes corresponds to the provisions of the treaty of peace and finds its foundation in that treaty. One adjustment in the boundary was made in 1850 when Britain ceded Horseshoe Reef in the Niagara River to the United States so that the latter could construct a lighthouse for the port of Buffalo.[4]

The designation by the Commissioners of the "middle" of the lakes as the international boundary not only provided an equitable division of the water resources but was also in conformity with existing rules of international law as indicated in the writings of Grotius and Vattel.[5] During the early part of the nineteenth century, the middle was considered to be a line equidistant from the opposite shores.[6] It was not until the twentieth century with the introduction of more precise cartographic techniques that a more exact meaning was assigned to the term and the boundary demarcated with precision on accurate maps.

The use of the equidistant line to determine the middle of the lakes was compatible with the rule of international law and acceptable to both the United States and Britain because it provided for an equitable sharing of the water resources and would not deny to either party adequate navigation rights. Application of the same line to the rivers and channels connecting the lakes was difficult and resulted in several disputes between the United States and Britain during the first decades of the nineteenth

Digest of the International Arbitrations to Which the United States Has Been a Party (Washington: Government Printing Office, 1898), I, 179; and U. S., Congress, House, *Boundary between the United States and Great Britain,* 25th Cong., 2d Sess., 1838, Exec. Doc. 451, p. 19. For the Steuben-Webster copy of Mitchell's Map which shows the red line draft of the boundary through the Great Lakes, see David Hunter Miller, ed., *Treaties and Other International Acts of the United States of America* (Washington: Government Printing Office, 1933), III.

    4. 18 *Stat.* (2) 325.

    5. Vattel writes: "If a lake lies between two States, it is held to be divided between them by a line through the middle of the lake." *Le Droit des Gens,* Book I, chap. xxii, sec. 274. See also Grotius, *De Jure Belli ac Pacis,* Book II, chap. iii, sec. xviii.

    6. David Thompson, astronomer and surveyor to the Commission, indicated that the boundary line adopted under Article VI was "as near as possible, equidistant from the opposite main shores; and whenever this line intersected an island, the island was considered as belonging to the side on which the greatest portion of it lay." See Document 451 (cited in n. 3, *supra*), p. 119.

century. Although not as colorful or controversial as the disputes involving the Alaskan boundary and the Northeastern frontier, the disputes over certain portions of the connecting rivers did involve enunciation and application of new rules of international law. Strict application of the equidistant line as the boundary was either impossible in certain cases because of islands located in the rivers or undesirable to the American authorities because it would locate the navigable channels in Canadian territory. In these disputes the British authorities invoked the *lex lata* and called for an application of the equidistant line as the "middle" with appropriate adjustments for intersecting islands. The United States authorities called for an application of what has come to be known as the *Thalweg* rule, but was in the early decades of the nineteenth century still a principle *de lege ferenda*.[7]

To resolve their boundary disputes the two governments looked to the use of joint commissions—a practice that had been inaugurated with the Jay Treaty of 1794. (These joint commissions are the antecedents of the present day International Boundary Commission and the International Joint Commission.) In the Treaty of Ghent (1814), the governments authorized the establishment of a two-member Commission to demarcate the international boundary through the lakes in conformity with the true intent of the treaty of peace and to provide a more precise delineation of the boundary than that incorporated in the initial treaty. In the event of a disagreement, the Commissioners were to submit separate reports with a subsequent reference to be made to a third party for a final settlement.[8] The Treaty of Ghent did not, however, enumerate the rules to be utilized by the Commissioners in their demarcation of the boundary. Moreover, the Commissioners were unable to agree upon the applicable customary rules of international law since the British authorities invoked the

7. See J. Cardozo's opinion in *New Jersey* v. *Delaware*, 291 U. S. 361.
8. 8 *Stat.* 218. For the text of the final report of the Commission, under Article VI, given on June 18, 1822, see 18 *Stat.* (2) 300. For a general summary of the Commission's work under Article VI, see Moore, *op. cit.*, I, 162–170; and see *ibid.*, VI, for copies of the maps prepared by the Commission under Articles VI and VII. For the joint report under Article VII, see *British and Foreign State Papers*, LVII, 803–823. For the final separate reports indicating their disagreements, see Document 451 (cited in n. 3, *supra*); and Moore, *op. cit.*, I, 171–195.

lex lata and the American authorities called for the application of principles *de lege ferenda*. They did, however, agree to one basic rule—the boundary should be a water line and no island should be divided between the two parties.[9]

Subsequently, however, both Commissioners presented what they considered to be the rules that had in fact governed the deliberations of the Commission. The American Commissioner (Porter) believed that the following rules had been utilized in practice, although not formally approved by the Commissioners: (1) the boundary line from St. Regis on the St. Lawrence River to Lake Superior should be a water line; (2) where there was only one navigable channel, it should be utilized without reference to its size or its contiguity to one or the other shore; (3) where there were two navigable channels, the boundary line should be designated through the one having the greater quantity of water; (4) where there were three or more channels, the line should pass along the one nearest the center, provided good navigation would be available to each party; and (5) where there was no navigation, the line should be drafted with reference to a fair division and proper location of the territory.[10]

For his part, the British Commissioner (Barclay) believed that the rules which had been accepted by the Commission were: (1) islands intersected by a middle line measured equidistant between the main shores were to be allocated in extent of quantity as equally as possible between the two parties; and (2) when an island was bisected into two unequal parts, the state on whose side the larger portion lay could elect to have the whole island and the party having the smaller portion would get credit for its share in the further allocation of the islands.[11]

To support his contention that the term "middle" as used in the treaties and by writers on international law meant a line equidistant from the opposite shores, the British Commissioner cited Vattel, Grotius, and von Martens and quoted them to the effect that a lake situated between two countries was to be divided by

9. Moore, *op. cit.*, I, 166; and Document 451 (cited in n. 3, *supra*), p. 9.
10. *Ibid.*, p. 5.
11. *Ibid.*, p. 119.

an equidistant line. For additional evidence he referred to an unperfected treaty (negotiated by Lord Hawkesbury and Mr. King in 1803) wherein the phrase "middle of the channel of the river" was used to indicate a portion of a boundary. This indicated, he declared, that if a channel were to be the boundary, the term "channel" would be employed; the term "middle of the river" was insufficient to mean the channel.[12] Reiterating Vattel's admonition that one should not interpret what was not in need of interpretation, he concluded:

The true and only reasonable interpretation [of "middle"] is this: the terms used in reference to lakes, can apply only to the equidistant line between the shores, for they cannot be said to have channels; and the same word applied without modification to rivers must bear the same construction, namely, the equidistant line between the banks of the river.[13]

The value of an equidistant line was that it could

be established as remote as possible, and at equal distances from the respective main shores; and it would thus afford that very muniment which is the direct intention of a water or arcifinious boundary; and, at the same time, it would be reduced to sufficient certainty, being established by distance defined by, and subject to, ocular demonstration.[14]

While accepting the equidistant line as the boundary for the lakes, the American Commissioner declared that it was inappropriate for the connecting rivers and called for the use of the navigable channel as the boundary.

The first and most ready interpretation of the phraseology here used by the parties, would seem to point to a line run longitudinally through this water communication, in such a direction as to be always midway or equidistant from the two opposite shores. Were this chain of water communication straight and of uniform size, or its shores but moderately curved and irregular, and, at the same time, were it free

12. For additional support Barclay could have cited the treaty between the United States and Spain, Oct. 27, 1795. Article IV provided that the boundary between the United States and Louisiana should be "the middle of the channel or bed of the River Mississippi." 18 *Stat.* (2) 704.
13. Document 451 (cited in n. 3, *supra*), p. 66.
14. *Ibid.*, p. 67.

from islands, this equidistant line might conveniently be, and probably would have been, adopted as the boundary. But a moment's inspection of the maps accompanying this report will exhibit much irregularities in the size, shape, and direction of this body of water, as to render the application of this principle inconvenient and ridiculous, if not utterly impracticable.[15]

There is yet another rule or principle for determining what is the middle of a river or water communication, not dependent, however, on scientific calculation, but adopted as a convenient, practical, and technical interpretation by writers on international law [his sole reference to international law in the discussion]. By this principle, the middle of a river is determined to be, along the thread of the channel or *filum aquae*, without reference to the relative distance from the opposite shores, or the quantity of water on either side. The reason and spirit of this rule are particularly applicable to a great portion of the boundary under the 6th and 7th articles of the Treaty of Ghent; and it has been very uniformly observed, in fact if not in form, by my colleague and myself, in tracing those parts of the line to which it is thus applicable. But it loses its value and application in cases (which often occur) where the river or water communication divides itself into two, or perhaps ten channels, not essentially variant either in size or depth, and each having its *filum aquae*.[16]

The two basic disputes that concerned the Commissioners involved the ownership of several islands in the mouth of the Detroit River and the ownership of St. George Island and the location of the boundary line through the Neebish Channels between Lakes Huron and Superior.

In the first dispute, the United States rejected the British contention that Bois Blanc, Sugar, and Stony Islands, in the mouth of the Detroit River, be given to Canada on the ground that if the latter obtained Bois Blanc the only navigable channel would be between that island and the Canadian mainland and thus wholly within Canadian jurisdiction. Although the British expressed confidence that if the dispute were taken to a third party their position would be maintained, they agreed to American ownership of Sugar, Fox, and Stony Islands with the boundary line through the channel between those islands and Bois Blanc on the

15. *Ibid.,* p. 5.
16. *Ibid.,* p. 7.

Canadian side. The British made this concession rather than break off the negotiations and incur the expense and delay of a reference to a third party.[17]

In the dispute concerning the Neebish Channels, the American Commissioner, referring to the principles which he declared had guided the Commission in its work, urged that the boundary line be fixed through the Eastern Neebish Channel since it was the only one of the three channels suitable for navigation. In contrast the British Commissioner, also referring to the principles which he said had governed the operations of the Commission, declared that the boundary should be fixed through the Middle Neebish Channel in accordance with the treaty stipulation that the boundary line was through the "middle" of the lakes and water communications. Since such a line would divide St. George Island into two parts (Canada having the larger part), the island should go to Canada with the United States receiving compensatory territory elsewhere. (If this rule were applied, the navigable channel would be wholly within Canadian jurisdiction.) In support of his contention, he pointed out that in the St. Lawrence River the Long Sault Islands and Barnhart Island had been awarded to the United States with the result that the only descending navigable channel was wholly within American jurisdiction.[18]

The Commissioners were unable to resolve the Neebish Channel dispute and the boundary line in that area remained in doubt until the Webster-Ashburton Treaty, despite the treaty provision that any dispute should be referred to a friendly sovereign for a solution. The final settlement incorporated in the Webster-Ashburton Treaty fixed the boundary line through the Eastern Neebish Channel, the navigable channel. In addition it was agreed that navigation of the channels in the St. Lawrence River near Barnhart Island, in the St. Clair River, and between Bois Blanc

17. *Ibid.*, p. 120. See also Joseph Delafield, *The Unfortified Boundary*, ed. Robert McElroy and Thomas Riggs (New York: privately printed, 1943), pp. 52 ff.

18. For the explanation of their respective positions concerning the dispute, see Document 451 (cited in n. 3, *supra*).

and the Canadian mainland would be free and open to the citizens and subjects of both parties.[19]

With the perfection of this treaty the boundary line through the entire Great Lakes system was agreed upon and established. Considering the existing state of cartography, the charts and the definition of the international boundary were as precise as could be expected. Agreement by the British and American governments that the middle of the navigable channel was the proper location for the boundary in the connecting rivers doubtless contributed to the development of the *Thalweg* as a customary rule of international law.

Delineation of the Present Boundary

Because of improvements in cartographic techniques and more extensive surveying, the boundary charts prepared in the early nineteenth century were by the twentieth century inadequate and in some cases inaccurate. Their inadequacy was highlighted in 1906 when a comparison of the official British Admiralty and U. S. Hydrographic charts revealed that they were not in agreement on the location of the international boundary through Lake Erie.[20]

Subsequent to this revelation, the matter of the Lake Erie boundary was referred to the International Waterways Commission (which had been established by the United States and Great Britain to investigate uses of the Great Lakes waters).[21] In its

19. 8 *Stat.* 572. For a record of the negotiations preceding the treaty, see *The Diplomatic and Official Papers of Daniel Webster, while Secretary of State* (New York: Harper, 1884), pp. 57–62, 114–147. For copies of the maps signed by Webster and Ashburton with the delineation of the boundary as they agreed to it, see Moore, *op. cit.*, VI, maps 26 and 35. Article II also fixed the boundary from Isle Royale to the mouth of the Pigeon River and thence up that river to Lac la Pluie. The Commissioners were unable to agree on that portion of the boundary when they could not locate the Isles Phelipeaux or the Long Lake as specified in the treaty of 1783. For details of this dispute, which is not material here, see Document 451 (cited in n. 3, *supra*), pp. 32 ff.

20. Comparison of the charts occurred as a result of the seizure by a Canadian patrol vessel of fishing nets purportedly placed in the American waters of Lake Erie. In reply to the offer of the Canadian patrol captain to assist the fishermen in marking the boundary, the Department of State indicated that such action would be merely a local *modus vivendi* and not a permanent demarcation of the international boundary. See Department of State file 460 (National Archives).

21. See *infra*, pp. 72–74 for the work of the Commission.

special report on the lake boundary the Commission explained that the contours of the lakes were unknown to the Commissioners in the nineteenth century; consequently the charts they prepared were inadequate for current requirements.

Their report explained that the term "middle" as incorporated in the treaties of 1783 and 1814 could mean any one of three possible principles: (1) a line being at all points equally distant from each shore, (2) a line following the general lines of the shores and dividing the surface water area as nearly as practicable into two equal parts, or (3) a line along the mid-channel dividing the navigable portion of the lake, and being at all points equally distant from the shoal water on each shore. The Commission indicated, however, that it was possible to delineate a boundary line that would not differ to any great extent from any of the above definitions, be in accordance with the treaties of 1783 and 1814, and consist of a minimum number of straight lines. Furthermore, it recommended that it be authorized to delineate the international boundary through the lakes from the St. Lawrence River to the Pigeon River on modern charts with reference to fixed monuments in accordance with the treaties of 1783, 1814, and 1842.[22]

As a result of the Commission's recommendations, Britain and the United States concluded a treaty in 1908 authorizing the accurate delineation of the international boundary through the Great Lakes. It was agreed that the boundary, delineated by the

22. For the text of the report, Jan. 4, 1907, see Canada, *Sessional Papers*, XLVII (1913), No. 12, Paper 19a, pp. 576–580. The utility of the Commission's interpretation of "middle" has been challenged by S. Whittmore Boggs, *International Boundaries: A Study of Boundary Functions and Problems* (New York: Columbia University Press, 1940), pp. 178–184. Boggs has included several diagrams to illustrate the fallacies in the various definitions proposed by the International Waterways Commission. Under the first definition lines would be drawn from one shore to the nearest point on the opposite shore. Then the midpoint would be connected. Using this procedure it is geometrically impossible to obtain only one "middle" line. Furthermore the results obtained by measuring from the opposite shore would be quite different. Under the second definition, any number of lines could be prepared which would allot one-half of the area to each side. The third definition is inapplicable since there are no channels in question. Having rejected these definitions, he suggests that the "middle" be defined as a line that is equidistant from the nearest point or points on opposite shores of the lake. Geometrically only one such line could be drafted. Consequently the median line would have a precise connotation. Boggs includes a diagram illustrating the difference between the present straight line boundary in Lake Erie and the line in accordance with his definition.

International Waterways Commission, would be recognized as the international boundary. Moreover it would consist of a series of straight lines wherever practicable.[23]

It is apparent that the Commission regarded its task of delineating the boundary as a technical matter to be accomplished by cartographers and surveyors. To facilitate its task it produced a series of thirty new charts projected on the new United States standard datum. (These charts vary in scale from 1:10,000 to 1:300,000 and show the standard features plus the boundary line.)

The present boundary line through the lakes was adopted in 1913. It does not follow the exact center of each body of water but consists of 270 straight lines that approximate a median line.[24]

The maintenance of the international boundary through the lakes is the responsibility of the International Boundary Commission established by the United States and Canada in 1925. This Commission supervises and maintains the entire boundary and considers all questions relating to it. It consists of two commissioners—one appointed by each country—and several technical assistants.[25]

23. The Canadian International Boundary, April 11, 1908. 35 *Stat.* 2003. See Appendix C.
24. International Waterways Commission, *Report of the International Waterways Commission upon the International Boundary between the Dominion of Canada and the United States through the St. Lawrence River and the Great Lakes* (Ottawa: Government Printing Bureau, 1916).
25. Boundary Treaty, Feb. 24, 1925. 44 *Stat.* 2102. See also Don C. Piper, "The Role of Intergovernmental Machinery in Canadian-American Relations," *South Atlantic Quarterly*, LXII (1963), 552–553.

3

Jurisdiction

The customary rules of international law provide that a state exercises complete jurisdiction over all territory and waters within its boundaries. With the designation of the middle of the Great Lakes as the international boundary, these lakes came under the respective jurisdictions of the United States and Canada. They are thus national waters and not *territorium nullius*.[1] In a like manner and for the same reasons, there is no area of open air space above the Great Lakes. This air space is within the respective jurisdictions of the United States and Canada. Such jurisdiction is expressly provided for in municipal legislation and is recognized by multilateral convention.[2] Although the lakes are internal waters, they are, nevertheless, considered as high seas by both countries for the purpose of admiralty and criminal jurisdiction. Consequently the general principles and practices of admiralty law and the principles of international law relative to the exercise of criminal jurisdiction on merchant vessels which apply to vessels on the high seas apply to vessels on the Great Lakes. In this instance the application of the established principles of international law provides a legal regime for the Great Lakes that is both necessary and effective.

1. The question whether the waters of the Great Lakes beyond three miles are open seas has been raised by fishermen anxious to cross the international boundary in order to conduct their fishing operations. See the letter of Acting Secretary of State Uhl, May 23, 1894, in Moore, *Digest*, I, 672–674; and U. S., Congress, House, *Preservation of the Fisheries in Waters Contiguous to the United States and Canada*, 54th Cong., 2d Sess., 1897, Doc. 315, p. 16.

2. See 49 U.S.C. sec. 1508; and the Convention on International Civil Aviation, Dec. 7, 1944, T.I.A.S. 1591, wherein the contracting parties recognize the exclusive jurisdiction of the subjacent state over the air space suprajacent to the territorial waters under its jurisdiction.

Dominium

Even though the Great Lakes are, according to international law, national waters under the jurisdiction of the United States and Canada, the federal governments do not enjoy or exercise *dominium* over the lakes. The state and provincial governments own the waters and the lake beds and exercise a corresponding degree of jurisdiction over them.

In the United States, the eight riparian states (New York, Pennsylvania, Ohio, Illinois, Indiana, Michigan, Minnesota, and Wisconsin) possess, in their respective public capacities, the waters and lake beds within their territorial limits.[3] (The territorial limits of each of the mentioned states extends into the waters of the adjacent lake or lakes.)[4] Title to the waters and the beds is held for public purposes to the exclusion of private ownership. In this instance public ownership of the waters and beds of the Great Lakes rests on the common-law principle that the state owns the sea bed under the tidal waters within its jurisdiction. Although the lakes are non-tidal, they are public navigable waters and the same principle of public ownership applies.

The same common-law principle of public ownership of the waters and the beds of the boundary lakes also operates in Canada. Title to these waters and beds is vested in the Crown in the right of the Province of Ontario.[5]

3. The principle of state ownership of the lake beds is affirmed in the Submerged Lands Act of 1953. 67 *Stat.* 29. See also 65 *C.J.S.*, Navigable Waters, sec. 92; *Illinois Central Railroad* v. *Illinois*, 146 U. S. 387 (1892); and *Hilt* v. *Weber*, 233 N.W. 159 (1929); Moore, *Digest*, I, 672; and 56 *Am. Jur.*, Waters, sec. 52.

4. See for example the *Ohio Revised Code Annotated* (Page, 1959 Supp.), sec. 123.03, wherein it is stated that the State of Ohio possesses, for public use, the waters and the bed of Lake Erie within the boundaries of the state, extending to the international boundary. See also *Illinois Central Railroad* v. *Illinois*, 146 U. S. 387, 452 (1892); *Bowes* v. *City of Chicago*, 120 N.E. 2d 15 (1954); and *State ex rel. Squire* v. *City of Cleveland*, 82 N.E. 2d 709 (1948).

5. Ownership is vested in the Crown in the right of the Province of Ontario because it is the only riparian province. See *Dixon* v. *Snetsinger*, 23 U.C.C.P. 235 (1873); and *R.* v. *Moss*, 26 S.C.R. 322 (1896), wherein it was specifically declared that the title to soil of navigable waters was vested in the Crown in the right of the province and not in the right of the Dominion.

Although the eight riparian states and the Province of Ontario have title to the waters and lake beds, such title is held subject to the paramount authority of the federal governments in the matters of navigation and commerce.[6] Under both the United States Constitution and the British North America Act, 1867, the respective central governments possess plenary power in the fields of commerce and navigation. The waters of the lakes are public navigable waters because they are navigable in fact and provide a continuous chain of navigation and a highway for commerce. As such they are subject to the authority of the central governments in the matter of navigation.[7] As a result, local police regulations may not contravene federal regulations concerning navigation.[8]

The paramountcy of the federal governments does not, however, prevent the local governments from exercising their police power when it does not interfere with navigation. In this regard an Ontario court held that it could exercise jurisdiction over an American vessel charged with violating the local liquor laws. The court acknowledged that there was a rule of international law prohibiting a state from interfering with a foreign vessel navigating the high seas, a rule which was applicable to the Great Lakes, since they had been declared to be high seas, but found, nevertheless, that the American vessel was not exercising a right of innocent passage through Lake Huron (a right that was guaranteed by treaty) but was, instead, sailing to and from a Canadian port with the intention of violating the local liquor laws. Consequently the rule of international law was inapplicable in this instance. Moreover, the court declared, the provincial legislature intended to interfere with the rule of international law and the local court was bound to give effect to the legislative enactment.[9]

6. 56 *Am. Jur.*, Waters, secs. 190–200. See also *Leamy v. The King*, 54 S.C.R. 143 (1916).

7. U. S. Const., Art. I, sec. 8; B.N.A. Act, Art, 91, secs., 2 and 10. The test of navigability being whether waters are navigable in fact rather than whether they are influenced by the ebb and flow of the tide is stated in *The Daniel Ball*, 10 Wall., 563 (1870); and approved in *Lefaivre v. Attorney General of Quebec*, 14 Que. K.B. 115 (1904).

8. See for example *Fleming v. Spracklin*, 50 Ont. L.R. 289 (1921).

9. *Rex v. Meikleham.* 11 Ont. L.R. 336 (1905).

Admiralty Jurisdiction

The extension of United States and Canadian admiralty jurisdiction to the Great Lakes is a significant development that makes
it possible to apply the customary rules of international law relating to vessels on the high seas to vessels operating on the lakes.
This is one example of the riparian states' frequent use of the
customary rules of international law to regularize the legal regime
of the Great Lakes.

Under the ancient common-law rules, admiralty jurisdiction
was applicable only to the high seas and tidal waters. This rule
was steadfastly adhered to by the American courts until the middle of the nineteenth century with the result that events on the
Great Lakes were beyond the purview of American admiralty
jurisdiction.[10] In 1845 Congress authorized the District Courts to
exercise admiralty jurisdiction in matters of contract or tort involving vessels of twenty tons or more, enrolled and licensed for
the coasting trade, when employed in commerce and navigation
between ports and places in different states upon the Great Lakes,
in the same manner as they exercised jurisdiction in matters
arising on the high seas or tidal waters. The procedure and remedies were to be the same as under the regular admiralty jurisdiction with the parties possessing a right to seek a concurrent
remedy at common law, where it was competent to give it, or to
seek any concurrent remedy which might be available under the
laws[11] of any of the riparian states.

Within a few years after its enactment, the act was upheld by
the Supreme Court in *The Genesee Chief* case. The ruling declared that the admiralty and maritime jurisdiction of the United
States was not limited to the high seas and tidal waters but

10. See *The Steamboat Thomas Jefferson,* 10 Wheat. 428 (1825). See also
George C. Sprague, "The Extension of Admiralty Jurisdiction and the Growth of
Substantive Maritime Law in the United States since 1835," *Law: A Century of
Progress, 1835–1935* (New York: New York University Press, 1937), III, 294–341;
and Grant Gilmore and Charles L. Black, Jr., *The Law of Admiralty* (Brooklyn:
Foundation Press, 1957), pp. 28–29.
11. Act of Feb. 26, 1845, 5 *Stat.* 726.

extended to all public navigable lakes and rivers where commerce was carried on between different states or with a foreign nation.[12] Delivering the opinion of the court, Chief Justice Taney declared that the act of 1845 did not rest upon the commerce power of the Constitution for its validity but upon the fact that the Great Lakes and their navigable connecting waters were within the scope of the admiralty and maritime jurisdiction as it was known and understood in the United States when the Constitution was adopted. The Great Lakes, he pointed out, were in truth inland seas and the extent of admiralty jurisdiction was dependent not upon the tidal character of the waters but upon their navigable character.

As a result of this decision, the admiralty jurisdiction of the United States was recognized as extending to the Great Lakes, but its scope was uncertain and indefinite. In *The Hine* v. *Trevor*, the Supreme Court implied that the act of 1845 applied only to the Great Lakes and that it was a limitation of the admiralty and maritime powers granted under the Judiciary Act of 1789 in that it restricted jurisdiction to American coasting vessels of more than twenty tons, employed in commerce and navigation between ports in different states.[13] In *The Eagle* the Supreme Court finally declared that the act of 1845 was inoperative save for the provision regarding a jury trial in admiralty questions because the Court's decision in *The Genesee Chief* refuted the premise upon which the act was predicated—that the admiralty jurisdiction was dependent upon the tidal character of the waters. Consequently the District Courts, upon whom admiralty jurisdiction had been exclusively conferred by the Judiciary Act, 1789, could take cognizance of all civil causes of admiralty jurisdiction upon the lakes and their connecting waters as upon the high seas.[14]

The courts have subsequently declared that admiralty jurisdiction extends to the Welland Canal,[15] to the Detroit River,[16] and to

12. *The Propellor Genesee Chief et al.* v. *Fitzhugh et al.*, 12 How. 443, 453, 457 (1851).
13. 4 Wall. 555 (1866).
14. 8 Wall. 15 (1868).
15. *Scott* v. *The Propellor Young America*, 21 Fed. Cas. No. 12,549 (1856); and *The Avon*, 2 Fed. Cas. No. 680 (1873).
16. *La Casse* v. *Great Lakes Engineering Works*, 219 N.W. 730 (1928).

the Erie Canal.[17] Thus the admiralty jurisdiction of the United States extends to the Great Lakes, their connecting waters, and the canals which serve the lakes.[18]

As a general rule, trial of admiralty cases is by the court without a jury.[19] In the 1845 act, however, Congress stipulated that in any matter of contract or tort involving vessels of twenty tons or more enrolled and licensed for the coasting trade and employed in commerce and navigation between ports of different states on the lakes, the parties might ask for a jury trial for all matters of fact put at issue in the case.[20] When the Supreme Court declared the act to be inoperative in *The Eagle*, this provision was exempted; consequently it is operative at the present time.[21] This privilege has been held to be applicable only to the Great Lakes and their connecting waters and then only to such issues of fact as arise in cases of contract or tort; it is not available either to foreign vessels or to those trading between ports of the same state.[22] Furthermore, the courts have held that in cases where a jury is employed the decision of the jury in matters of fact is merely advisory and is not binding upon the court.[23] Because of its uniqueness, this provision for a jury trial has been criticized as introducing a "system of trial wholly foreign to the practice, forms, and procedure of the courts of admiralty."[24]

Canadian courts have also declared that the Great Lakes are similar to the high seas and thus within admiralty jurisdiction. This was first established in the *Queen* v. *Albert Sharp*, where the Court of Chambers declared that the lakes were within admiralty jurisdiction and that offenses committed on the lakes were as though committed on the high seas and within the jurisdiction of

---

17. *The Robert W. Parsons*, 191 U. S. 17 (1903).
18. *The Frank J. Fobert*, 32 F. Supp. 214 (1940); *Tyler* v. *Industrial Commission*, 158 N.E. 586 (1927).
19. 2 C.J.S., Admiralty, sec. 146.
20. See n. 11.
21. See 28 U.S.C. sec. 1873.
22. *The Western States*, 159 F. 354 (1908); *The City of Toledo*, 73 F. 220 (1896); *The Erie Belle*, 20 F. 63 (1883).
23. In *The Empire*, 19 F. 558 (1884), the court held that the judge could disregard the jury's decision if in his opinion it failed to do substantial justice. See also *The City of Toledo*, 73 F. 220 (1896).
24. *The Western States*, 159 F. 354 (1908).

the Canadian courts.[25] Subsequently the Dominion Parliament created the Maritime Court of the Province of Ontario to exercise jurisdiction over all cases arising out of or connected with navigation, shipping, trade, or commerce on the lakes or other waters of the province. The court did not, however, possess jurisdiction over criminal matters.[26] The court was subsequently abolished after the passage of the Colonial Courts of Admiralty Act and the designation of the Exchequer Court of Canada as the Colonial Court of Admiralty for Canada.[27] The Imperial statute which authorized the creation of the Colonial Courts of Admiralty provided that the new courts were to exercise jurisdiction similar to that of the High Court in England and to have the same regard to international law and the comity of nations. To carry out the Imperial mandate, the Dominion Parliament authorized the Exchequer Court to exercise admiralty jurisdiction over all Canadian navigable waters whether tidal or not. Jurisdiction extended to all rights and remedies in all matters arising out of navigation, shipping, trade or commerce.[28] Under the present Admiralty Act, the Exchequer Court continues to exercise similar jurisdiction. In addition, the court is empowered to exercise jurisdiction over claims for salvage services in relation to the salvage of life or property from aircraft on or over the Great Lakes.[29]

Notwithstanding the existence of an admiralty court, the Supreme Court of Ontario declared that it could entertain a suit for damages for negligence resulting from the collision of two vessels in inland waters since the jurisdiction of the admiralty court was merely concurrent and not exclusive.[30]

The scope of Canadian admiralty jurisdiction was raised in the case of the *D. C. Whitney.* The issue involved was whether an American vessel could be seized by the Canadian admiralty court while it was in the process of innocent passage through the Canadian channels of the Detroit River.[31] The *Whitney* had been

25. *The Queen* v. *Albert Sharp,* 5 Pr. R. 135 (1869).
26. Act of 1877 in Canada, *Rev. Stat.* (1886), c. 137.
27. Great Britain, *Statutes at Large,* 53 and 54 Vict., c. 27 (1890).
28. Canada, *Statutes at Large,* 54 and 55 Vict., c. 29 (1891).
29. Canada, *Rev. Stat.* (1952), c. 1, sec. 18 (1) and (5).
30. *Shipman* v. *Phinn,* 31 Ont. L.R. 113 (1914).
31. *The Ship D. C. Whitney* v. *The St. Clair Navigation Co.,* and *The Southern Coal and Transportation Co.,* 38 S.C.R. 303 (1907).

involved in a collision with another American vessel within American waters. Subsequently an attempt was made to seize the vessel as it passed through Canadian waters on a voyage from one American port to another. The Canadian court declared that the ship could not be considered as within Canadian admiralty jurisdiction when it was on a voyage of innocent passage through one of the Canadian channels that had been declared by treaty to be open to Canadian and United States ships. The court said in part:

I do not think that the *D. C. Whitney*, a foreign ship, while sailing from one port of a foreign country to another port of that country and passing through, in the course of her voyage, one of the channels declared by convention or treaty to be equally free and open to the ships, vessels and boats of both countries, can be said to be within any jurisdiction conferred on any Canadian court by the sovereign authority in the control of the Dominion of Canada, even though that channel happened to be Canadian waters.[32]

In a somewhat similar case the United States Supreme Court declared that Canadian admiralty law, not American admiralty jurisdiction, would govern the collision, in the American waters of Lake Superior, of two Canadian vessels that had unintentionally entered American waters.[33]

Criminal Jurisdiction

Since the international boundary passes through the middle of the lakes, the United States and Canada, as the territorial sovereigns, exercise criminal jurisdiction over that portion of the lakes within their borders. In addition, because the Great Lakes have been declared to be high seas for the purpose of criminal jurisdiction, each may exercise jurisdiction over offenses on board vessels of its flag even if the offense occurs on the other side of the

32. *Ibid.*, p. 309.
33. *Canada Malting Co., Ltd.* v. *Paterson Steamships Ltd.*, 285 U. S. 413 (1932). In this instance one of the cargo owners filed a libel *in personam* against an owner of one of the vessels while a suit was pending in the Canadian admiralty court to determine liability. The court declined to take jurisdiction on the ground that it could do so in controversies between foreigners arising in territorial waters.

international boundary. Consequently, certain offenders may be subject to concurrent jurisdiction.

The existence of concurrent criminal jurisdiction on the Great Lakes, following decisions by the courts of both countries that the lakes are to be considered as high seas, is consistent with the recognized principle of international law that a state may exercise jurisdiction over offenses committed within its territory and also over offenses committed upon vessels flying its flag, even if the vessel is within foreign territorial waters.[34] For an offense committed on an American vessel in Canadian lake waters, the offender is subject to Canadian and American jurisdiction. The former has jurisdiction because it is the territorial sovereign; the latter because it is the flag state. For an offense on a Canadian vessel in American lake waters, the offender is also subject to concurrent jurisdiction for the same reasons. In the United States, a riparian state rather than the federal government would exercise jurisdiction since the "special maritime and territorial jurisdiction" of the federal government extends only to American vessels. In any event, the decision as to which authority will in fact exercise jurisdiction generally depends upon the nature of the offense and the physical possession of the accused.

Under an Imperial statute, Canadian courts were authorized to exercise jurisdiction over offenses on the high seas or where the Admiral had power as if the offense had been committed within the local jurisdiction.[35] Pursuant to the statute, the Court of Chambers in *The Queen* v. *Albert Sharp* announced that the Great Lakes were within the admiralty jurisdiction and consequently the Ontario courts could exercise jurisdiction over an offense on the lakes even if the alleged offense occurred on the American side of the international boundary.[36] This decision es-

34. See *United States* v. *Flores*, 289 U. S. 137 (1933); *The Wildenhus Case*, 120 U. S. 1 (1887). C. John Colombos, *The International Law of the Sea* (4th rev. ed.; London: Longmans, 1959), pp. 275–280; and *Regina* v. *Anderson*, II Cox's *Criminal Cases*, 198 (1868).
35. Act of Aug. 1, 1849, Great Britain, *Statutes at Large*, 12 and 13 Vict., c. 96 (1849).
36. *The Queen* v. *Albert Sharp*, 5 Pr. R. 135 (1869). In this case, Sharp and another, both British subjects, were charged with scuttling a vessel on Lake Erie. It was not known whether the offense had been committed on the Canadian or American side of the boundary. The court declared that the specific site was

tablished the precedent that concurrent jurisdiction existed on the Great Lakes.

The Canadian Criminal Code, which is federal and not provincial, authorizes the courts of Ontario to entertain jurisdiction over criminal offenses on the Great Lakes when the offenses are committed on vessels employed on inland waters.[37] Previously the code also stipulated that proceedings for the trial of an alien charged with an offense committed within the admiralty jurisdiction might not be instituted in a Canadian court without the consent of the Governor General.[38] In clarifying this requirement, the court held that permission was unnecessary if the offense was committed on a foreign vessel while the vessel was within inland waters.[39] Under the revised criminal code official permission for the trial of aliens for offenses committed on Canadian lake waters is not necessary.

The American courts were much more reluctant to declare that there existed concurrent jurisdiction in criminal matters on the Great Lakes. In *The People* v. *William Tyler*,[40] decided a decade before the Canadian case, *The Queen* v. *Albert Sharp*, the Supreme Court of Michigan declared that the Great Lakes could not by any stretch of the imagination be considered as high seas. Justice Christiancy indicated that if the lakes were to be considered as high seas then the international boundary should have been extended only to the shores of the lakes and they should have been specifically exempted from the jurisdiction of either riparian state. Reviewing the peace treaty, 1783, the Jay Treaty, 1794, the Webster-Ashburton Treaty, 1842, and the Reciprocity

---

irrelevant since the lake was within the admiralty jurisdiction and the court could exercise jurisdiction even if the offense occurred on the American side of the boundary.

37. See the Revised Criminal Code, 1954, in Canada, *Statutes at Large*, 2 and 3 Eliz. II, c. 51, sec. 419 (1953–1954).

38. This provision was amended in the Revised Criminal Code to require the consent of the Attorney General for the local courts to try an alien for an offense, committed on a foreign vessel, within the three mile limit. Consequently the new provision is inapplicable to the Great Lakes. See *idem*, sec. 420 (2).

39. See *R.* v. *Furuzawa*, 1 W.W.R. 955 (1930).

40. 7 Mich. 160 (1859). Tyler shot one Henry Jones while on board an American vessel on the Canadian side of the St. Clair River. Jones was taken to Port Huron, Michigan, where he died of the wound inflicted by Tyler. One question before the court was whether Tyler was subject to federal jurisdiction. In this instance the court rejected federal jurisdiction.

Treaty, 1854, he concluded that the subjects and citizens of either party, while within the territorial waters of the other, were bound by the laws of the territorial sovereign according to the established principle of international law by which a state exercises exclusive jurisdiction over its territory. Both the United States and Great Britain, he declared, were estopped by the mentioned treaties from considering the lakes comparable to the ocean and the high seas. Chief Justice Martin supported his colleague, declaring:

When the constitution was formed, it cannot—except by the most violent presumption—be presumed that the lakes and their connecting waters were intended to be embraced within the admiralty jurisdiction of the United States. The term was employed in the sense it had been for centuries used in the mother country, and, from their first settlement, in the colonies, to designate jurisdiction upon the ocean—that space without the territorial limits of any government—in the common highway of all nations. The lakes, and rivers or straits connecting them, were not presumed to be of such a character.[41]

This view was subsequently reversed by the United States Supreme Court in *United States* v. *Rodgers*.[42] In this case the Court declared that the Great Lakes were to be regarded as "high seas" in the sense that an individual charged with committing an offense on board an American vessel while on the lakes could be tried and punished in the same manner as one charged with committing an offense upon an American vessel while on the high seas. Delivering the opinion of the Court, Justice Field announced that the term "high seas" should be interpreted in its true sense to mean the open and unenclosed waters of all seas, rather than in the old sense of the seventeenth century when it

41. 7 Mich. 163.
42. 150 U. S. 249 (1893). In 1888 Rodgers was charged with assault with a dangerous weapon on one Downs while on board an American vessel on the Canadian side of the Detroit River. He was tried under section 5346 of the U. S. *Rev. Stat.* which provided: ". . . every person who, upon the high seas, or in any arm of the sea, or in any river, haven, creek, basin or bay, within the admiralty jurisdiction of the United States, and out of the jurisdiction of any particular State, on board a vessel belonging to the United States, or any citizen thereof, with a dangerous weapon, or with intent to perpetrate any felony, commits an assault upon another, shall be punished. . . ."

was generally interpreted to mean the open waters of the ocean and seas surrounding Great Britain.

As thus defined, the term would seem to be as applicable to the open waters of the great Northern lakes as it is to the open waters of those bodies usually designated as seas. The Great Lakes possess every essential characteristic of seas. They are of large extent in length and breadth; they are navigable the whole distance in either direction by the largest vessels known to commerce; objects are not distinguishable from the opposite shores; they separate, in many instances, states, and in some instances constitute the boundary between independent nations; and their waters, after passing long distances debouch into the ocean. The fact that their waters are fresh and not subject to the tides, does not affect their essential character as seas.[43]

Prior to the Court's decision in the *Rodgers* case, but after Rodgers had committed the offense for which he was charged, Congress amended the federal penal code to provide specifically for federal jurisdiction over offenses on board American vessels "being on a voyage" upon the waters of any of the Great Lakes or any of the connecting waters.[44] In the revised penal code the same provision was included with the additional provision that federal jurisdiction would also extend to offenses committed upon American vessels while on a voyage through the international section of the St. Lawrence River.[45] The code did not require that the offense be committed within American waters but merely that it occur upon an American vessel on a voyage upon the Great Lakes; consequently the District Courts could exercise jurisdic-

43. *Ibid.*, pp. 256–257. The decision was not unanimous. Justice Grey strongly dissented, declaring: "The lakes are not high seas, for the very reason that they are inland seas, within the exclusive jurisdiction and control of those countries within whose territories they lie, or between territories they are the boundary; and therein essentially differ from the high seas, where the law of no particular State has exclusive force, but all are equal," *ibid.*, p. 271. See also Harry E. Hunt, "How the Great Lakes became 'High Seas' and Their Status Viewed from the Standpoint of International Law," *AJIL*, IV (1910), 285–313, where the writer decries the decision of the court in the *Rodgers* case and asserts that since there are no common or unappropriated waters on the Great Lakes and they contain no marginal sea, they cannot be considered as high seas. The writer also predicts that dire results will follow from the decision.

44. Act of Sept. 4, 1890, 26 *Stat.* 424. The new act did not, of course, affect the decision of the court in the *Rodgers* case.

45. 35 *Stat.* 1088.

tion over an offense committed on an American vessel while the vessel was within Canadian waters.

Since 1961 American vessels on the Great Lakes and their connecting waterways, plus the international section of the St. Lawrence River, have been designated as being within the "special maritime and territorial jurisdiction" of the United States for the purpose of criminal jurisdiction. The penal code stipulates that certain offenses are punishable by the federal courts if they are committed within this jurisdiction. It should be emphasized that as far as the Great Lakes are concerned, the special maritime and territorial jurisdiction extends not only to offenses committed on American vessels on the Canadian side of the international boundary but also to offenses on the American side of the boundary which would normally be the subject of state jurisdiction.[46]

In addition the code provides that when an offense, not specified in the penal code, occurs within the special maritime and territorial jurisdiction, the federal courts may assume jurisdiction if the offense is committed within the territorial limits of a state where it is an offense under the law of that state.[47] In *United States* v. *Gill*, the defendant was charged with an offense which was not a crime under the federal penal code but which was a crime under the law of Indiana. The District Court took jurisdiction in this instance because the offense occurred upon a vessel on a voyage on Lake Michigan while the vessel was within the territorial limits of the State of Indiana. In this same decision, the court also declared that the special maritime and territorial jurisdiction of the United States extended to vessels in transit between ports of Lake Michigan.[48]

As the result of a recent case, *Hoopengarner* v. *United States*, it appears that an offender may be subject to both federal and state jurisdiction for the same event occurring upon the Great Lakes. In this instance the court concluded that since the Detroit River was within the special maritime and territorial jurisdiction of the

46. 18 U.S.C. sec. 7. The listed offenses include such crimes as arson, assault, murder, and manslaughter.
47. 18 U.S.C. sec. 13. This is the so-called federal crimes assimilative provision.
48. 204 F. 2d 740 (1953).

United States, the fact that the defendant had been convicted by a state court for assault following a boat collision in the Detroit River did not prevent the federal government from trying him on another charge arising from the same set of facts.[49]

. . . . .

The opening of the St. Lawrence Seaway and the entrance of foreign ocean-going vessels into the lakes does not present any new problems of criminal jurisdiction for the riparian states. Because of the principle of territorial sovereignty, the appropriate Canadian or United States courts have the right of jurisdiction over any offense within their territory irrespective of the nationality of the vessel. In accordance with international comity, the courts would doubtless waive their right of jurisdiction over minor offenses relating to the internal discipline of the vessel. Whether other states regard the Great Lakes as similar to the high seas for purposes of their own admiralty and criminal jurisdiction is not known. Such a question might arise if the riparian state does not exercise jurisdiction over an offense committed on a vessel while on the lakes and the accused is returned to the flag state for trial. In this regard the practice of the United States and Canada in considering the lakes to be high seas for the purpose of admiralty and criminal jurisdiction would appear to be a useful precedent for such countries and would be compatible with the customary rules of international law.[50]

49. 270 F. 2d 465 (1959). Since there is but one criminal code in Canada, a federal code, there is little likelihood that an offender would be indicted by two jurisdictions.

50. See n. 34.

· 4 ·

Regulation and Preservation
of the Fishery

Commercial fishing on the Great Lakes, doubtless practiced by
the Indian tribes and the early settlers, has developed into a
business that is ideally situated to serve the largest population
concentration in North America. The lakes are the principal domestic source of whitefish, lake trout, walleye, blue pike, yellow
perch, chubs, and ciscoes. Although the catch of food fish in the
lakes has declined during the past decade, the annual catch usually totals more than one hundred million pounds and is valued at
more than ten million dollars.[1] In 1960 approximately 5,700 people were engaged in commercial fishing on the lakes.[2] Since the
fish do not recognize the necessity for or existence of an international boundary, the optimum development and protection of the
food fish is a binational rather than a national problem. Although
the International Pacific Halibut Commission and the International Pacific Salmon Fisheries Commission have been very successful for over three decades in protecting and developing valuable species of food fish for the benefit of Canadian and United
States fishing interests, it has been only within the past decade
that all the interested parties have been able to agree upon and
establish for the Great Lakes an international fisheries commission with modest authority.[3] The establishment of an international
regime for the lakes is a complex matter, for it requires the co-
operation of the two federal governments, the eight riparian
states, and the Province of Ontario. Failure to establish the re-

1. U. S. Department of Interior, Bureau of Commercial Fisheries, "Great Lakes
Fisheries, 1963." C.F.S. No. 3624. (Mimeographed.)
2. *Great Lakes Newsletter*, March, 1962, p. 4.
3. See Don C. Piper, "The Role of Intergovernmental Machinery in Canadian-
American Relations," *South Atlantic Quarterly*, LXII (1963), 556–564.

gime precluded for many years any effective action to combat the depletion of commercially valuable food fish by either federal government. Many of the efforts of the present international commission are directed toward resolving problems that should have been corrected years ago.

Although the Great Lakes are considered by both governments to be high seas for the purpose of admiralty and criminal jurisdiction, they are not high seas for the purpose of fishing. Both the United States and Canada have emphasized their right under international law to exclude foreign fishing vessels and to maintain strict control over the fishery within their respective waters. The possibility of open fishing beyond a three-mile limit was raised during the last decade of the nineteenth century but was quickly rejected by authorities from both countries.[4] Moreover, the treaties that guarantee to citizens of both countries the right to cross the international boundary for the purpose of trade and commerce do not include a right to cross the boundary in order to fish within the territorial waters of the other party.[5]

In the United States, ownership of the fish and control of all fishing activities on the lakes is vested in the eight riparian states. As a result the American waters are divided into eight sections under the jurisdiction of eight different authorities, each of which establishes its own commercial fishing policy and promulgates its own laws and regulations.[6] The division of authority and the

4. In 1894 the Department of State indicated: ". . . this Government can neither claim nor admit that in the center of these lakes, on either side of the treaty boundary, and up to a distance of one marine league from shore, there can be an area of 'high seas'. . . ." Moore, *Digest*, I, 672. In the same year a Canadian court in *The Grace* declared:

"Upon the ocean the law of nations recognizes the limit of three marine miles from shore as the only portion of the ocean in respect of which a state can claim to exercise territorial rights; but the same law of nations recognizes the authority of a state to claim the same territorial rights in respect of so much of all inland lakes as lie within the limits of its conventional boundaries. If a foreign vessel, therefore, is twenty miles from shore, and is fishing without a license a quarter of a mile north of the boundary line upon an inland lake, she is subject to seizure and condemnation. . . ." 4 Ex. C.R. 283, 289 (1894).

5. See Moore, *Digest*, I, 674; and *For. Rel.* (1880), pp. 493–494. In 1917 the State Department denied that there was any treaty giving Canadian Indians living on Cornwall Island a right to fish on the American side of the boundary. Department of State file 711.428/436 (National Archives).

6. In Lakes Erie and Michigan four separate codes control the United States fishery. See 36 *C.J.S.*, Fisheries, secs. 6, 7, 19, 28; 22 *Am. Jur.*, Fish and Fisheries,

division of powers which excludes direct federal involvement more than any other factor precluded for many years the establishment of an international regime.

In Canada the situation is somewhat less complex. Although ownership of the fish in the lakes is vested in the Province of Ontario, the federal government under the British North America Act is authorized to issue regulations regarding the inland fisheries.[7] As a result the federal government issues regulations governing commercial fishing on the lakes that are administered by the Ontario Department of Lands and Forests. The regulations issued by the Governor in Council doubtless represent the views and desires of the Ontario authorities. Since all of the Canadian lakes are within the Province of Ontario, uniform fishing regulations are applicable to all Canadian waters.[8]

Commercial fishing on the lakes is licensed by the appropriate state or provincial authority. Each of the riparian states and the Province of Ontario has set forth as a matter of public policy certain requisites for the issuance of a commercial fishing license. These requisites are not pertinent here except insofar as they relate to the issuance of licenses to non-residents or aliens. In this regard aliens do not receive national treatment.[9] The Province of Ontario as a matter of policy does not issue commercial fishing licenses to non-residents. American fishing fleets are thus excluded completely from Canadian lake waters.[10] In the United

---

sec. 17; *Lincoln* v. *Davis*, 19 N.W. 103 (1884); *Stuart* v. *Greanvea*, 117 N.W. 655 (1908), where the court declared that the right to fish, like the right to navigate, is a public right which extends to all parts of the Great Lakes. See also *Winous Point Shooting Club* v. *Slaughterbeck et al.*, 117 N.E. 162 (1917); and *Kuehn* v. *City of Milwaukee*, 53 N.W. 912 (1892).

7. Section 91 (12). See the decision of the Judicial Committee of the Privy Council in *Attorney General for Dominion of Canada* v. *Attorneys General for the Provinces of Ontario, Quebec, and Nova Scotia*, A.C. 700 (1898).

8. Ontario Fisheries Regulations, P.C. 1954–160, SOR/54–36. See also Canada, House of Commons, Standing Committee on Marine and Fisheries, *Minutes of Proceedings and Evidence*, No 1, Bill 279 (1955), pp. 1, 17, 25.

9. For a convenient summary of the fishing regulations, see Great Lakes Fisheries Commission, "Summary of Laws Relating to Commercial Fishing on the Great Lakes" (1962), pp. 38–42. (Mimeographed.)

10. Licenses are issued by the Ontario Department of Lands and Forests, although under the Fisheries Act and the Coastal Fisheries Protection Act the federal government has the authority to promulgate regulations regarding the issuance of commercial fishing licenses. See Canada, *Statutes at Large*, 9–10 Eliz. II, c. 23; 1–2 Eliz. II, c. 15; and the Ontario Fisheries Regulations cited in n. 8, *supra*. Under an act of 1868 (Canada, *Statutes at Large*, 31 Vict., c. 61) Parliament

States the pattern of treatment varies. The states of Ohio, Pennsylvania, and Minnesota restrict commercial fishing operations to citizens of the United States.[11] The states of Wisconsin, Illinois, and New York permit the issuance of non-resident licenses without specifically stating that non-residents must be United States citizens.[12]

The states of Michigan, which exercises jurisdiction over parts of the fishery in Lakes Erie, Huron, Michigan, and Superior, and Indiana, which exercises jurisdiction over the fishery in a small area of Lake Michigan, do grant commercial fishing licenses to aliens. Under the statutes of both states, Canadian fishermen may be issued non-resident licenses to fish for commercial purposes. During 1960 ten commercial fishing licenses were issued to Canadian residents for commercial fishing operations in the Michigan waters of Lake Huron and two licenses for commercial fishing in the Indiana waters of Lake Michigan.[13]

Violations of the state or provincial licensing regulations by foreign fishing vessels have occurred in the past and occasionally

authorized the Governor General to grant licenses to foreign vessels to fish in Canadian waters, including inland waters. In 1870 the license system was terminated and all foreign fishermen were thenceforth excluded from fishing in Canadian waters. See *For. Rel.* (1870), p. 408. During the negotiations for the Treaty of Washington (1871), Sir John A. Macdonald insisted that American citizens should not be given the right to fish in Canadian lake waters since they would not abide by the fishing regulations. See Joseph Pope, *Memoirs of the Right Honorable Sir John Alexander Macdonald* (Ottawa: Durie and Son, n.d.), II, 100.

11. See *Ohio Revised Code Annotated* (Page), sec. 1533.35. *Minnesota Statutes Annotated*, sec. 98.45 (5) and 98.46 (2). In 1930 the Minnesota Attorney General declared that a Canadian citizen could not lawfully conduct commercial fishing operations in the Minnesota waters of Lake Superior. He also indicated that the fact that only American citizens could obtain commercial fishing licenses did not prohibit licensed fishermen from employing aliens to assist in fishing operations. *Ibid.*, sec. 102.28. See also *Purdon's Pennsylvania Statutes Annotated*, Title 30, sec. 90. In addition sec. 92 provides that no commercial fishing license may be issued to a resident of any state or country which does not grant fishing licenses to Pennsylvania residents. Since Canada does not issue licenses to American fishermen for lake fishing, this provision serves to prevent Canadians from fishing in the Pennsylvania waters of Lake Erie.

12. *Wisconsin Statutes* (1957), sec. 29.33; *Illinois Annotated Statutes* (Smith-Hurd), c. 56, sec. 230; *Consolidated Laws of New York*, Conservation Law, sec. 210.

13. Canadian fishermen do not receive national treatment regarding the fee for a commercial fishing license. *Compiled Laws of the State of Michigan* (1948), c. 308, secs. 23a and 24; *Mason's Michigan Supplement* (1956), c. 308; *Annotated Indiana Statutes* (Burns, 1956), sec. 11–1413; and letters from D. Robson, Chief, Field Administration Division, Michigan Department of Conservation, Dec. 19, 1960; Kenneth Marlin, Director, Indiana Department of Conservation, Jan. 3, 1961.

still occur.[14] Although some of the violations of the international boundary are intentional, the majority are probably unintentional[15] and due in part to the fact that the international boundary is not physically demarcated through the lakes. For the most part known violations are handled by the local courts or in some cases by diplomatic exchange of notes. Apparently in only one instance has there been a formal diplomatic claim as a result of the seizure of a fishing vessel on the Great Lakes.

In the case of *The Grace*, a Canadian court ordered the American vessel forfeited to the Crown for fishing on the Canadian side of Lake Erie without a license. In delivering its opinion, the court emphasized that it was "an axiom of International Law that every state is entitled to declare that fishing on its coast is an exclusive right of its own subjects."[16] In similar cases, vessels and gear have been released when the appropriate court was uncertain whether the seizure had occurred within its jurisdiction.[17]

Occasionally patrol vessels have erroneously and illegally seized fishing vessels or equipment operating in another jurisdiction. In one such incident the Canadian government expressed its regrets for the inadvertent seizure by one of its patrol vessels of American fishing nets in the United States waters of Lake Erie. Although the Department of State accepted the Canadian government's apology, it advised the owners that if they were unable to conclude a settlement with the Canadian authorities for the damages suffered as a result of the incident they could file a claim against Great Britain with the Department. The Department, of course, did not promise to present the claim but merely to give it consideration consistent with existing international relations.[18]

14. Within the past decade there have been reports of the arrest and conviction of Canadian fishermen for fishing in the Ohio waters of Lake Erie. See *New York Times*, May 10, 1957, p. 53; March 26, 1959, p. 22.
15. See Department of State file 711.428/1971, 1973 (National Archives).
16. 4 Ex. C.R. 283, 288 (1894).
17. In *Rex v. The Kitty D*, 2 Ont. W.R. 1065 (1903), the court wisely foresaw "as regards contentious jurisdiction, there is a question about arresting a ship, but this expedient seems not to be desirable, because it might easily be abused and would be exceedingly apt to lead to a small warfare of jurisdiction." In some cases the Canadian court, when in doubt as to the location of the seizure, has refused to take jurisdiction. See Department of State file 711.428/845 (National Archives).
18. In this instance the Department of State asked the Canadian authorities to make the investigation. It was subsequently discovered that the Canadian police captain had erred in his position and had himself violated the international

In the case of the *R. T. Roy*, the State Department did present a diplomatic claim to Great Britain for $3,578.35 for damage arising out of the seizure of the American fishing vessel on Lake Huron in 1908. The claim was presented to the British-American Claims Tribunal established under the 1910 agreement. The question of fact presented to the Tribunal was whether the seizure had occurred on the American or Canadian side of the international boundary. Here the Tribunal found that it was faced with an "irreconcilable conflict of untested and untestable statements." The Tribunal declined to consider the fact at issue and disallowed the claim on the ground that the claimant had not utilized the Canadian legal remedies that were open to him. In taking this action, the Tribunal pointed out that under the provisions of the Terms of Submission one of the equities which the Tribunal could take into consideration was any failure on the part of the claimant to obtain satisfaction through the legal remedies which were placed at his disposal. The American Agent (Nielsen) objected to the disallowance, pointing out that the Terms of Submission also provided that no claim should be disallowed or rejected by the Tribunal on the application of the general principle of international law requiring exhaustion of local remedies. Perhaps the Tribunal's action, although of doubtful legal validity, may be explained in part by its desire to avoid the necessity of resolving the conflicting statements of fact.[19]

---

boundary. See Department of State file 711.428/605–607, 619 (National Archives). The claim would have been presented to the United Kingdom since in 1920 direct diplomatic relations had not been established between Ottawa and Washington.

19. See *Report of Fred K. Nielsen, American and British Claims Arbitration* (Washington: Government Printing Office, 1926), pp. 408–410. The vessel and crew had been arrested and taken into a Canadian port, where preliminary statements were taken. Subsequently the vessel was escorted by a Canadian vessel to a second port, where the judicial proceedings were to be held. During the trip the *R.T. Roy* went aground. The escort vessel continued to seek assistance. During its absence, the crew of the *R.T. Roy* was able to release the vessel and returned with it to Michigan waters. Thus there were no Canadian proceedings concerning the seizure.

Art. III of the Terms of Submission, July 6, 1911, governing the presentation of claims, provided: "The Arbitral Tribunal shall take into account as one of the equities of a claim to such extent as it shall consider just in allowing or disallowing a claim, in whole or in part, any failure on the part of the claimants to obtain satisfaction through legal remedies which are open to him or placed at his disposal, but no claim shall be disallowed or rejected by application of the general

The International Regime

The international regime for the conservation and control of the food fish of the Great Lakes was finally created in 1955 with the establishment of the Great Lakes Fisheries Commission. Such a regime, for many years considered to be desirable and necessary, was slow in coming into being primarily because of the opposition of the commercial fishing industry and unwillingness of the riparian states and the Province of Ontario to relinquish any of their control over the fishery. Despite its slow birth, an international regime was inevitable. For many years there had been a depletion of the food fish in the lakes as the result of overfishing and the unwise use of gill nets. In addition, beginning in 1940 the parasitic sea lamprey began to take its toll of the lake trout and whitefish, the most valuable of the lake fish.[20] Both developments emphasized the need for a systematic, co-ordinated, and inclusive binational effort.

Suggestions for some type of joint co-operation and control by the riparian states were voiced as early as 1875. In the period from 1883 to 1943 over twenty-seven formal and informal conferences were held to discuss the problems of the Great Lakes fishery. Many of these conferences were inter-state but some were attended by representatives from Canada.[21]

The first formal bilateral action was taken in 1892 when the

---

principle of international law that the legal remedies must be exhausted as a condition precedent to the validity of the claim." *Ibid.*, p. 9.

20. As a result of the sea lamprey, the U. S. lake trout catch on Lake Huron fell from 1,743,000 lbs. in 1935 to 50 lbs. in 1951. In Lake Michigan the catch was 6,800,000 lbs. in 1943; by 1952 it was only 3,000 lbs. The loss to U. S. fishermen is estimated to be $3,500,000 per year. U. S., Senate, Subcommittee of the Committee on Foreign Relations, *Hearing, Great Lakes Fisheries Convention,* 84th Cong., 1st Sess., 1955, p. 10.

21. See L. Larry Leonard, *International Regulation of Fisheries* (Washington: Carnegie Endowment for International Peace, 1944), pp. 115–118; and International Board of Inquiry for the Great Lakes, *Report and Supplement* (Washington: Government Printing Office, 1943), pp. 30–34. See also "Poor Fish—in the Great Lakes," *State Government,* XI (1938), 51–52; and Elmer Higgins, "Fish Outlive Officials," *State Government,* XI (1938), 53–54, 58. When discussions took place between representatives of Pennsylvania and Canada in 1907, the State Department insisted that any formal agreement would have to be left to the international treaty powers; Pennsylvania was not a plentipotentiary. See Department of State file 8275/1 (National Archives).

United States and Great Britain established a joint Commission to
investigate the fishery in the waters contiguous to the two countries. The Commission made several recommendations, including:
(1) the establishment of a permanent joint Commission to be
charged with the direct supervision of the fishery, (2) the promulgation of a uniform system of regulations for each body of
water along the entire boundary, and (3) the delineation of the
international boundary line through the lakes' waters in order to
remove a source of annoyance and irritation. In addition, the
Commission prepared specific technical recommendations for
each of the lakes and waters under investigation.

Although both governments were to examine the Commission's
recommendations to appraise the expediency and practicality of
concluding a convention or promulgating concurrent legislation
to give them effect, the only recommendation that was implemented was the delineation of the international boundary.[22]

Apparently one of the difficulties precluding the conclusion of a
treaty regulating the fishery was the claim by the state governments of exclusive control over the fishery and Canadian uncertainty as to the authority of the United States federal government
to enforce the proposed regulations.[23] To clarify the federal government's authority, Attorney General Griggs in 1898 stated that
the regulation of the fishery in the boundary waters between the
United States and Canada was a proper subject for a treaty and
that although a treaty might supersede state laws its legal validity
would not be impaired.[24]

Because most of the Commission's recommendations were not
implemented, joint control and regulation of the fishery was one
of the topics on the agenda for the Joint High Commission
(1898–1899) appointed to resolve the outstanding problems between the United States and Canada.

22. For the appointment of the Commission, see *For. Rel.* (1892), pp. 317,
324–326. For its report, see U. S., Congress, House, *Preservation of the Fisheries in
Waters Contiguous to the United States and Canada,* 54th Cong., 2d Sess., 1897,
Doc. 315.
23. See the memorandum from the Canadian government, Dec. 21, 1905, in
Governor General file, R.G. 7, G. 21, No. 192 A, Vol. I (a) (Public Archives of
Canada).
24. 22 *Ops. Atty. Gen.* 214.

A Commission subcommittee discussed the matter and prepared a draft treaty, which, with some changes, was subsequently perfected in 1908 by the United States and Great Britain.[25] The treaty provided for the establishment of the International Fisheries Commission with responsibility for the preparation of uniform international regulations for the protection and preservation of the food fish, including such matters as the extent of the open season, the size and use of nets, and provisions for concurrent measures for the propagation of food fish.[26]

Under the provisions of the treaty the regulations were to apply to the waters of the Great Lakes excluding Lake Michigan and Georgian Bay in Lake Huron. Although the United States desired to include Georgian Bay within the scope of the treaty, it did not press the matter since it wished to avoid any question concerning Lake Michigan, believing that "the exercise of jurisdiction by the treaty making power of the United States over waters entirely surrounded, as Lake Michigan is, by United States territory would present a more complicated question than that arising in the case of boundary waters, and for that reason it would be as well to avoid it."[27]

The parties agreed to put the regulations into operation and enforce them by appropriate legislative and executive action with commensurate penalties for violations. Each government would exercise jurisdiction over offenders found within its territorial waters regardless of nationality, as well as over its own citizens

25. See Governor General file R.G. 7, G. 21, No. 192 A, Vol. I (a) (Public Archives of Canada).

26. Fisheries in United States and Canadian Waters, April 11, 1908. 35 *Stat.* 2001.

27. While the question might be complicated, it was certainly not insurmountable. Britain suggested that Lake Michigan be included within the scope of the treaty since it had been included within the proceedings of the International Waterways Commission. The State Department was convinced that the Canadians wanted to balance Georgian Bay against Lake Michigan in the adjustment of rights and interests in the use of boundary waters. If the waters of Georgian Bay could be classed as tributary waters rather than as a part of the boundary waters, it might be of some future advantage to Canada. (In 1909 the Boundary Waters Treaty was concluded.) The United States insisted that Lake Michigan should be excluded since it was wholly within American territory. See Department of State file 8275/2-3 (National Archives). Secretary of State Root told Lord Bryce that the same regulations that applied to the other lakes would in fact apply to Lake Michigan and that the desire to exclude the lake from the scope of the treaty lay in sentiment rather than in any practical effect. See Governor General file, R.G. 7, G. 21, No. 192 A, Vol. I (b) (Public Archives of Canada).

found within its jurisdiction who had violated the regulations within the waters of the other party.

Eighteen specific regulations were adopted by the Commission to be applied to the treaty waters and were submitted to the governments.[28]

It appears from the correspondence regarding the preparation of the regulations that the United States federal government intended to promulgate the regulations and authorize enforcement by state authorities. In addition the states would be free to adopt other regulations that were neither in conflict nor inconsistent with the purposes of the regulations and the treaty. The question whether any specific state regulation was in conflict with the federal regulations would be a matter for determination by the courts. In response to an inquiry from the Canadian government regarding the enforcement of the regulations, the State Department indicated that, since each party had agreed to put the regulations into force, whether they were enforced by federal or state authorities was unimportant.[29]

Although the President could have promulgated the regulations by executive action, they were submitted to Congress for its approval. They were subsequently approved by the Senate, but the House of Representatives refused to take any action. As a result, they were never promulgated by the President.[30] Because of American inaction, in 1914 Britain abrogated the treaty and Canada resumed its freedom of action with regard to fishery regulations.

28. For the text of the report and the regulations, see U. S., Congress, House, *Protection and Preservation of Food Fishes in International Boundary Waters of the United States and Canada*, 61st Cong., 2d Sess., 1910, Doc. 638. The regulations included provisions for such matters as type of species which might be taken, size of nets, and the use and location of nets.
The regulations were assailed by some state authorities as absurd and were criticized as having been prepared by persons who had no knowledge of Great Lakes problems. Department of State file 711.428/195 (National Archives). See also Department of State file 8275/75–76 (National Archives).
29. Department of State file 8275/2–4, 53–54, 58–59 (National Archives).
30. See Hackworth, *Digest*, I, 799; Department of State file 711.428/336, 395 (National Archives). The Canadian government took the position that no body other than the International Fishery Commission had authority to amend or modify the regulations. It further insisted that there was no reason why the regulations should be submitted to Congress prior to presidential promulgation. Department of State file 711.428/240 (National Archives).

Despite the failure of the 1908 treaty, United States federal officials and private authorities were convinced in the 1920's and 1930's that the conclusion of a formal treaty between the United States and Canada was the only workable and effective method for the control and preservation of the Great Lakes fishery. The treaty was considered a more effective instrument than the interstate compact because of the cumbersomeness of the instrument and the difficulty of enforcement.[31] It was realized that perfection of a treaty would be difficult because of the primacy of state authority and the open opposition from the Province of Ontario and the commercial fishing interests in the United States.[32]

Finally in 1940, as a result of the urging of the Council of State Governments, Canada and the United States established the International Board of Inquiry to consider and recommend measures for the conservation of the lakes' fishery. The Board conducted extensive hearings and prepared five general recommendations with regard to joint investigation of the fishery.[33]

In a supplementary report the members of the American section considered the appropriate means to obtain joint co-operation in the control and preservation of the fishery in the light of the repeated failures of the riparian states to enact uniform legislation or to accept informal agreements concluded as a result of interstate conferences. They agreed that an interstate compact was undesirable because of the difficulty of negotiations and because Canada would not be a party.[34] Consequently they rec-

31. See Department of State file 711.428 Great Lakes/33, 44 (National Archives). In 1928 Secretary of Commerce Hoover indicated that an international treaty appeared to be the only way to prevent the complete exhaustion of the fishery. He advocated the deferment of treaty negotiations until there was a more insistent demand for international control to ensure the perfection of a treaty. Department of State file 711.428/1032, 1323 (National Archives).

Secretary of State Hull opposed the use of an interstate compact declaring: "I am satisfied that the existing method of making treaties constitutes the more appropriate method of regulating this phase of foreign relations." See International Board of Inquiry for the Great Lakes Fisheries, *Report and Supplement* (Washington: Government Printing Office, 1943), p. 35.

32. Department of State file 711.428 Great Lakes/36, 55, 61 (National Archives).

33. See 54 *Stat.* 2409. For the recommendations which included, *inter alia,* that there be common investigation of the fisheries and that there be adequate statistics on the fisheries, see Board of Inquiry, *op. cit.,* pp. 23–24.

34. See *ibid.,* pp. 36–38.

ommended that a conservation treaty similar to that concerning migratory birds be utilized. This type of treaty was preferred to the halibut or salmon conventions because of the difficulty of determining the composition of a joint commission.[35]

Notwithstanding the American section's recommendations, the United States and Canada signed in 1946 a comprehensive treaty similar to the halibut and salmon conventions. The treaty provided for the establishment of the International Commission for the Great Lakes Fisheries, consisting of an American and a Canadian section with an advisory committee for each lake. The Commission was to have extensive authority in directing the preparation of regulations concerning the open and closed seasons, the open and closed waters, the limits for the catch of each species, and the type and use of fishing gear. The regulations prepared by the Commission would not be effective until approved by the President and Governor in Council, which gave the executive in each federal government a veto. The regulations were to be enforced in the first instance by the Province of Ontario and the riparian states within their respective waters. If there were complaints as to the effectiveness of the enforcement, the federal government concerned would take appropriate measures to ensure proper enforcement. Although Lake Michigan was within the scope of the treaty, the United States section alone would exercise the Commission's functions relating to that lake.[36]

Opposition from the commercial fishing industry to the Commission's authority to regulate fishing operations was immediate

35. Both the halibut and the salmon conventions provide for the establishment of a joint commission. For a discussion of their activities see Don Piper, *South Atlantic Quarterly*, LXII, 557–562.

No joint commission was established under the migratory bird convention; the two parties merely agreed to take the necessary measures to ensure the execution of the convention. See 39 *Stat.* 1702. Composition of a possible joint commission for the Great Lakes involved the question whether the eight riparian states should be members, thus necessitating a commission of sixteen members, or whether the commission should be kept small. If the latter, how would the American members be selected and what representation, if any, would the riparian states have on the commission?

36. For the text of the unperfected treaty, see U. S., Congress, Senate, *Convention with Canada for the Development, Protection, and Conservation of the Fisheries of the Great Lakes*, 79th Cong., 2d Sess., 1946, Ex. C.

and intense. As a result the President withdrew the treaty from the Senate and did not ratify it.[37]

After two unsuccessful treaties and several joint studies, the United States and Canada were finally able in 1954 to conclude and perfect a treaty establishing an international regime with limited authority. Following the pattern of the halibut and salmon conventions, the treaty establishes the Great Lakes Fisheries Commission consisting of two national sections of three members each.[38] Representation of the riparian states is accomplished by their membership on national advisory committees for each lake. Unlike the halibut and salmon treaties and commissions, the Great Lakes treaty and Commission relate to all species of fish and not just a particular species.

The Commission's stated task is to promote and co-ordinate research to conserve the lake fishery and to formulate and implement a comprehensive program for the control and eradication of the sea lamprey. As a result of its research program, the Commission is to recommend various measures to the contracting parties, but it has no authority to put the recommendations into force. Unlike the proposed 1946 convention, the Commission has no regulatory authority over the fishery.[39]

The treaty specifically provides that it does not change the established rights and jurisdiction over the fishery held by the riparian states, the federal government of Canada, and the Province of Ontario. For the United States, recommendations for conservation measures that are prepared by the Commission are forwarded by the Secretary of State to the riparian states for such action as they think appropriate.[40] Since the federal government

37. Because of the intense opposition, the Senate Foreign Relations Committee did not even conduct hearings on the treaty; see *Hearings* cited above in n. 20, at p. 9.

38. During the hearings on the convention, the Deputy Undersecretary of State (Murphy) declared that the convention "adapts our successful Fishery Commission experience to Great Lakes needs and to the legal situation that the waters in concern are State waters and not territorial waters or high seas." See *Hearings* cited above in n. 20, at p. 7.

39. For the text of the treaty, see 6 U.S.T. 2836. See also Charles B. Selak, Jr., "The United States—Canadian Great Lakes Fisheries Convention," *AJIL*, L (1956), 122–129.

40. 16 U.S.C. sec. 939. Henry Reiff writes: "Whoever devised the Great Lakes Fisheries Convention and the American statute enforcing the same could have spared Solomon many an anxious moment as he proceeded to judgment upon

promulgates the fishing regulations, the troublesome problem of the division of governmental powers is not relevant in Canada.

Unlike the earlier unperfected treaties, the present convention applies to all of the Great Lakes and the international section of the St. Lawrence River. Furthermore, the United States section does not possess any authority to act unilaterally with regard to Lake Michigan.

During the first half-decade of its existence, the Commission concentrated its efforts primarily on programs for the control and eradication of the sea lamprey and the rehabilitation of the lake trout. In recent years, however, the Commission has broadened its scientific activities. It has also undertaken studies of the desirability, feasibility, and probable effect of uniform fishing regulations for all waters of the Great Lakes. In this regard it has only the power of persuasion.[41]

Whether the scope of the Commission and the international regime will be expanded in the future depends not only on the effectiveness and usefulness of the Commission, but also on the resolution of American constitutional questions involving federal participation in a matter which is primarily within state jurisdiction. If the American states are unable to co-operate or agree on a uniform fishing code under the present treaty venture, survival of the fishery would seem to demand federal intervention via the treaty power (as was resorted to with respect to migratory birds) and the expansion of the international regime. Co-operative action by all riparian governments is a necessity if the fishery is to be preserved.

---

babies and other equally indivisible entities." *The United States and the Treaty Law of the Sea* (Minneapolis: University of Minnesota Press, 1959), p. 293. In statements before the House of Commons, the Minister of Fisheries (Sinclair) indicated his belief that the states had surrendered their authority over the fisheries to the federal government. This would seem to be an erroneous reading of the treaty; it certainly seems inconsistent with the mentioned section of the U. S. Code. Canada, House of Commons, *Parliamentary Debates*, 1955, pp. 2242–2244, 4019.

41. Great Lakes Fisheries Commission, *Annual Report*, 1962, p. 11.

Navigation Rights and Practices

A cursory look at the map of North America shows immediately that the Great Lakes are a major artery of transportation and commerce. Major population centers and industrial complexes rim the lakes and provide the base for an extensive network of regional waterborne transportation. Within the past decade the regional network has been expanded to a worldwide system with the completion of the St. Lawrence Seaway. This extensive navigation network is built upon a foundation of bilateral treaties and agreements and concurrent legislation that provides an effective legal regime for the entire Great Lakes—St. Lawrence system. In viewing this legal regime, three aspects must be considered. The first is the complex of treaty arrangements between the United States and Canada that guarantees to the nationals of each state the right of open and unimpeded navigation of the entire system. These arrangements have been of great importance because until the opening of the St. Lawrence Seaway, navigation on the lakes was essentially a bilateral matter. The second aspect is a new but important development that is a consequence of the opening of the seaway and relates to the rights of vessels of third states to enter and navigate the St. Lawrence and the Great Lakes. The privileges and benefits to be accorded such vessels are not set forth in precise terms in any bilateral arrangement between the United States and Canada. The third aspect concerns the specific practices that govern and facilitate navigation on the lakes, such as the rules of the road, salvage and wrecking rights, and load line regulations. Some of these practices are set forth in treaties, others in exchanges of notes, and others are specified in co-ordinated municipal legislation.

Navigation Rights of the Riparian States

The open, unimpeded navigation of the entire Great Lakes— St. Lawrence system has been a matter of concern to the United States and Canada (or Great Britain) since the first days of American independence. The present bilateral legal regime is the result of negotiation and compromise rather than the application of *a priori* legal principles. It was not accomplished by one single agreement; rather it involves navigation rights in three areas each of which must be considered separately: the boundary waters, the St. Lawrence River, and Lake Michigan.

The boundary waters. The treaty of peace of 1783 which drew the international boundary through the middle of Lakes Ontario, Erie, Huron, and Superior, and part of the St. Lawrence River, contained no provision for the reciprocal navigation of the Great Lakes without concern for the international boundary. That such a provision was not included is somewhat surprising in light of Article VIII, which provided for the open and unimpeded navigation of the Mississippi River from its source to the ocean.[1] Subsequently such a provision was included in the Jay Treaty (1794). Article III of that treaty guaranteed to the citizens or subjects of each party the right to navigate the lakes and rivers of the other party for the purposes of trade and commerce without reference to the international boundary. This right of free and open navigation apparently applied only to the contiguous waters and did not encompass either the Canadian section of the St. Lawrence River (i.e. above the 45th parallel) or the waters of Lake Michigan.[2]

Although both American and Canadian courts have declared, in this twentieth century, that Article III of the Jay Treaty was

1. This provision was apparently included in the erroneous belief that the Mississippi River had its source near the new international boundary.
2. 8 *Stat.* 116. Although the provisions concerning navigation were to be in force for a period of only twelve years in Jay's initial draft, they were fortunately incorporated into the permanent articles in the perfected treaty. See Samuel Flagg Bemis, *Jay's Treaty, a Study in Commerce and Diplomacy* (New York: Macmillan, 1923), p. 299.

abrogated by the War of 1812,[3] the free and open navigation of the boundary waters continued throughout the nineteenth century with the Jay Treaty as the apparent legal foundation. Vessels of both parties navigated the lakes without reference to the boundary. In addition, the British Navigation Code, which required that goods being imported into British ports be carried in British bottoms, was not enforced on the lakes, with the consequence that Canadian lake ports were open to American vessels. In the 1820's several Imperial statutes were enacted which specifically permitted American vessels to bring certain goods (primarily agricultural) into Canadian ports. Although these statutes legitimated a practice which had become commonplace, they imposed a duty on the American goods that had theretofore been admitted duty-free.[4]

Notwithstanding the right of free and open navigation of the boundary waters incorporated into the Jay Treaty, freedom to navigate the boundary lakes was an important consideration in the delineation of the international boundary by the Commissioners appointed under Articles VI and VII of the Treaty of Ghent and in the settlement of the remaining boundary disputes in 1842. In the final settlement of the Webster-Ashburton Treaty a boundary line incorporating the *Thalweg* principle was adopted.[5] In addition the treaty provided that the channels in the St. Lawrence River on both sides of the Long Sault Islands and Barnhart Island (the navigable channels were on the American side of the boundary), the channels in the Detroit River on both sides of Bois Blanc (on the Canadian side of the boundary) between that island and both the American and Canadian shores, and the channels and passages lying near the various islands at the junc-

---

3. See *Karnuth v. United States ex rel. Albro*, 279 U. S. 231 (1929); and *Francis v. The Queen*, [1955] 4 D.L.R. 760.

4. Of the eighty schooners operating on Lake Erie in this period, no more than ten were British owned and manned. See David R. Moore, "Canada and the United States, 1815–1830" (Chicago: Press of Jennings & Graham, 1910), p. 107. See also D. C. Creighton, *The Commercial Empire of the St. Lawrence, 1760–1850* (Toronto: Ryerson Press, 1937), pp. 236, 358–370; the opinion of the Law Officer, Lower Canada, June 1, 1824, in Canada, Archives, *Documents Relating to the Constitutional History of Canada, 1819–1828* (Ottawa: Patenaude, 1935), pp. 225–228; Great Britain, *Statutes at Large*, 3 Geo. IV, c. 119; *ibid.*, 6 Geo. IV, c. 114; *ibid.*, 6 Geo. IV, c. 73.

5. See above, pp. 14–15.

ture of the St. Clair River and Lake St. Clair should be free and open to the vessels of both parties.[6]

Thus until the first decade of the twentieth century, reciprocal navigation on the boundary lakes and the natural waterways from the Pigeon River to St. Regis on the St. Lawrence was guaranteed by the Jay Treaty and the Webster-Ashburton Treaty. These treaty provisions were replaced in 1909 by the comprehensive Boundary Waters Treaty that is presently in force. That treaty guarantees "forever" to the inhabitants and vessels of both parties the free and open navigation of all navigable boundary waters. It is significant that in contrast to the earlier treaties, the privileges of this treaty are not restricted to subjects and citizens but are available to "inhabitants and vessels" of both parties, which would apparently encompass alien *amis* resident within either the United States or Canada. In addition the absence of the word "subject," which had been incorporated into the earlier treaties, would seem to preclude British subjects not inhabitants of Canada from enjoying the privileges of the treaty. Notwithstanding the perpetual nature of the navigation provision, both parties possess the right to promulgate laws or regulations that are applied equally and without discrimination and are not inconsistent with the privilege of free navigation.[7]

It should be noted that although the treaty guarantees navigational rights, navigation is not considered to be the most important use for the boundary waters. Article VIII stipulates the following order of precedence for the use of the boundary waters: (1) uses for domestic and sanitary purposes, (2) uses for navigation, including the service of canals for the purposes of navigation, and (3) uses for power and for irrigation. No use of the waters is to be permitted which tends materially to conflict with

---

6. 8 *Stat.* 572, Arts. II and VII. The provision that navigation should be free and open is understood to mean that there must be equality of rights regarding navigation. This does not preclude the imposition of tolls or charges for improvements so long as such tolls or charges are applied without discrimination. See *Pigeon River Co. v. Cox Co.*, 291 U. S. 138 (1934); and *Arrow River and Tributaries Slide and Boom Co., Ltd. v. Pigeon Timber Co., Ltd.*, [1932] S.C.R. 495.

7. Art. I. See Appendix E. Although the treaty was signed by the British Ambassador, James Bryce, the actual negotiations were conducted by a Canadian, George Gibbons.

or restrain any other use which is higher in the order of precedence.

Notwithstanding the secondary importance assigned to navigation, the treaty provides that although each party may make provisions for water diversion within its territory, the other party may object if the diversion is productive of "material injury" to the navigational interests within its territory. Each party also possesses the right to construct works for the benefit of commerce and navigation provided they do not adversely affect the flow of the boundary waters or the water level on the other side of the boundary.[8]

Thus there has been since 1794 treaty foundation for the open and unimpeded navigation of the boundary lakes of the Great Lakes and the international section of the St. Lawrence River. Since that time there have been only a few minor differences regarding the navigation rights in the contiguous waters. Several of the disputes have related to the legality of the Canadian government's granting exclusive international ferry franchises between certain ports. Objections to the franchises were raised on the ground that such exclusive grants violated the right of free navigation guaranteed by the pertinent treaties.[9]

Lake Michigan. Since neither the Jay Treaty nor the Webster-Ashburton Treaty granted to British subjects the right to navigate Lake Michigan, navigation of the lake was, and still is, considered

8. This matter is discussed more fully below, see pp. 74–77.

9. For information on this matter, which was raised in the 1920's, see Department of State file 711.42155 Ferries/1–57 (National Archives). In 1884 the United States protested the action of the municipal authorities of Sarnia, Canada, in granting exclusive ferry privileges between that town and Port Huron, Michigan, and excluding Americans from engaging in ferry operations between the two ports. In its protest the United States insisted that navigation of the boundary waters by vessels of both parties was guaranteed "on an entirely free and equal footing." *For. Rel.* (1884), pp. 243–245, 255.

One incident concerning the right of navigation remained unsettled for over one hundred years. It involved the seizure of the British schooner the *Lord Nelson* on the waters of Lake Ontario on June 5, 1812—two weeks before the commencement of the War of 1812. Although the seizure was declared illegal by a United States court in 1817 and the United States subsequently admitted its liability, no compensation was paid the owners for over a century. In 1914 the British-American Claims Tribunal ordered payment of $5,000 for the value of the vessel plus interest at four per cent for its use. See Report of Fred K. Nielsen, *American and British Claims Arbitration* (Washington: Government Printing Office, 1926), pp. 432–435.

as a separate matter, apart from the navigation of the boundary waters. British subjects first obtained a treaty right to navigate the lake in the Reciprocity Treaty (1854). This right was conditional, being predicated on the continuance of the American treaty right to navigate the Canadian section of the St. Lawrence River and was to remain in force so long as the latter right remained in force. Both privileges, however, lasted for only a decade and were terminated in 1866 when the United States abrogated the treaty.[10]

Subsequently provisions for the navigation of the lake were incorporated in the Treaty of Washington (1871). This time the right of navigation was extended for a period of ten years, subject to two years' notification of termination. Navigation of the lake for the purpose of commerce was subject to all laws and regulations of the federal government and the riparian states not inconsistent with the right of free navigation.[11]

Since the treaty did not specifically grant to British subjects national treatment, they were required to fulfil American customs regulations before entering Lake Michigan.[12]

A more permanent basis for the right of Canadian vessels to navigate Lake Michigan is set forth in the Boundary Waters Treaty. So long as that treaty remains in force, the guaranteed right of navigation that obtains for the boundary waters also obtains in like manner for Lake Michigan. Thus Canadian navigation on Lake Michigan is a conditional and not a perpetual right. All laws and regulations relative to navigation must be applied equally and without discrimination to the citizens of both parties.[13] This national-treatment provision, incorporated for the first time in the 1909 treaty, required a change in the American cus-

10. 10 *Stat.* 1089, Art. IV.
11. 18 *Stat.* 355, Art. XXVIII. During the treaty negotiations, the Canadian Commissioner, Sir John A. Macdonald, insisted that navigation of the lake should be a reciprocal concession for navigation of the Canadian section of the St. Lawrence River. See Joseph Pope, *Memoirs of the Right Honourable Sir John Alexander Macdonald* (Ottawa: Durie and Son, n.d.), II, 128–129. See also *For. Rel.* (1873), III, 402–404.
12. See Governor General file, R.G. 7, G. 21, No. 130, Vol. 5 (b) (Public Archives of Canada).
13. Art. I. In the treaties of 1854 and 1871, navigation of Lake Michigan was extended to British subjects. Under the 1909 treaty this privilege is available only to inhabitants and vessels of Canada.

toms laws. The requirement that Canadian vessels stop at a customs station was terminated on the ground that it was in conflict with a specific provision of a self-executing treaty.[14]

The St. Lawrence River. Although free and open navigation of the boundary waters was initially guaranteed by treaty in 1794, a treaty provision relating to the free and open navigation of the Canadian section of the St. Lawrence River (i.e., above the 45th parallel) was not agreed upon until the middle of the nineteenth century.[15] When the treaty privilege was finally extended, it was accompanied by a *quid pro quo* from the United States.

In 1794 John Jay raised the question of navigation on the St. Lawrence with the British authorities, but they were unwilling to accept any treaty provision on the subject. On the contrary, Article III of the treaty contained a reservation which served to prohibit American navigation of the St. Lawrence except for small vessels trading between Quebec and Montreal.[16]

The question of free navigation of the river did not become a matter of real concern to the United States until the 1820's. Under an Imperial statute of 1790, American goods were imported into Canadian ports and then exported to Great Britain as Canadian goods without the payment of any duty.[17] Furthermore, since the navigation code was not enforced upon the lakes, American vessels could enter Canadian lake ports with American goods. In 1822 the Imperial Parliament enacted two statutes which in effect legally permitted American vessels to navigate the Canadian section of the St. Lawrence in order to import certain goods into Canadian ports. For the first time, however, the American goods were subject to a duty; furthermore the provincial governor had the authority to designate which ports, if any, would be open to American vessels.[18]

In order to offset the effects of the import duty imposed as a

14. See Department of State file 711.42146/2, 9, 10 (National Archives).
15. See Ruth E. Bacon, "British and American Policy and the Right of Fluvial Navigation," *BYIL*, XIII (1932), 76–92.
16. Henry P. Johnston, ed., *The Correspondence and Public Papers of John Jay* (New York: Putman, 1893), IV, 124.
17. Great Britain, *Statutes at Large*, 30 Geo. III, c. 29.
18. *Ibid.*, 3 Geo. IV, chaps. 44 and 119.

result of the new statutes, the United States asserted that its citizens had a natural right to navigate the St. Lawrence River from the Great Lakes to the ocean.[19] In making this assertion, the United States was convinced that the right of navigation could be established upon the "sound and general principles of the Law of Nature."[20] Secretary of State John Quincy Adams explained the American position:

We know that the possession of both of the shores of a river at its mouth, has heretofore been held to give the right of obstructing or interdicting the Navigation of it to the people of other Nations, inhabiting the banks of the river above the Boundary of that in possession of its mouth. But the exclusive right of jurisdiction over a river originates in the social compact, and is a right of nature, preceding it in point of time, and which the sovereign right of one Nation cannot annihilate, as belonging to the people of another.[21]

To support its argument, the United States, with occasional citations to Vattel and Grotius, suggested additional reasons why its citizens had a right to navigate the St. Lawrence River. These included the fact that nature intended for her gifts to be used by all people, that the river was in fact a strait connecting two large bodies of water (the ocean and the Great Lakes) and none could deny the right of the United States to navigate these bodies, that the right of navigation had been jointly acquired by American citizens with the British since the United States was a part of the Empire when Great Britain acquired the Canadas, and that free navigation was necessary for the conduct of trade and

19. H. A. Smith points out that the comprehensive arguments by the United States for the right to navigate the entire St. Lawrence River to the ocean were in fact irrelevant since the river did not provide a continuous waterway to the ocean and commercial navigation was physically impossible. He asserts that the primary concern of the United States was not navigation but free entry of American goods into Canadian ports. *Great Britain and the Law of Nations* (London: P. S. King, 1935), II, 320, 347.

20. William R. Manning, *Diplomatic Correspondence of the United States: Canadian Relations* (Washington: Carnegie Endowment for International Peace, 1942), II, 36. The United States was not the first government to assert a natural right to navigate a river flowing through the territory of another state. In 1792 the Executive Council of the French Republic opened the Scheldt River and based its argument in part on natural law. See S. T. Bindoff, *The Scheldt Question to 1839* (London: Allen and Unwin, 1945), p. 143.

21. Manning, *op. cit.*, II, 36. Although the diplomatic notes are enlightening, a detailed discussion of the various arguments is not material here. For the basic papers, see *ibid.*, II, 413–430.

commerce as recognized by the major European powers at Vienna in 1815 in opening the Rhine, Maine, Neckar, Moselle, Meuse, and Scheldt rivers.[22]

The British authorities met the American argument with "immediate, positive, unqualified resistance," but indicated a willingness to discuss it "on principles of accommodation and mutual concession." Basing their rejection on the right of property and the belief that any right of passage must be restricted to innocent utility, the British declared:

. . . mere convenience and the profits of trade cannot be deemed to constitute that case of extreme necessity under the Law of Nations, to which the rights of Property may perhaps be occasionally required to give way. It has already been shewn that such interests can at most amount to an imperfect right of innocent utility, the exercise of which is entirely dependent on the will and discretion of the local Sovereign.[23]

The navigation question was moderated in the 1830's when the British abolished the duty on American goods imported into Canada and established several duty-free ports where American export goods could be stored. When the question again came under consideration in the late 1840's and early 1850's, Canada was in economic difficulty as a result of the abolition of the colonial preferences in 1846 and the construction of the Erie Canal and the Buffalo-Albany railroad, all of which served to divert goods to New York, where they were then exported to Europe. To obtain a reciprocity treaty with the United States, Canada was willing to offer the navigation of the St. Lawrence River.[24]

22. See *ibid.,* II, 81–82; *American State Papers, Foreign Relations,* VI, 757 ff.; and *Hertslet's Commercial Treaties,* I, 3, for the text of Art. 108 of the General Treaty signed in Congress at Vienna, June 9, 1815.
23. Manning, *op. cit.,* II, 412, 423–430.
24. For a discussion of the background of the Reciprocity Treaty, see Creighton, *op. cit.,* p. 367; James M. Callahan, *American Foreign Policy in Canadian Relations* (New York: Macmillan, 1937), pp. 242–262; Charles C. Tansill, *The Canadian Reciprocity Treaty of 1854* (Johns Hopkins University Studies, 1922); and U. S., Congress, House, *Reciprocal Trade with Canada,* 31st Cong., 1st Sess., 1850, Doc. 64. During the discussion of reciprocity, the assertion of a natural right to navigate the St. Lawrence was revived, but a House Committee took the position "if it [navigation of the St. Lawrence] cannot be secured as a right, then it is to be considered as a privilege, to be acquired either by treaty or by some reciprocal legislation, based upon the idea of rendering a just equivalent." See U. S., Congress, House, *Free Navigation of the St. Lawrence,* 31st Cong., 1st. Sess., 1850, Rept. 295, p. 20.

Consequently the Reciprocity Treaty (1854) granted the privilege of navigation of the Canadian section of the river to the "citizens and inhabitants" of the United States "as fully and freely as the subjects of Her Britannic Majesty." The grant was not perpetual, for the British authorities retained a right to suspend it. If the privilege were suspended, the United States had the right to suspend the reciprocity provisions relative to Canadian goods.[25]

Although the treaty was abrogated by the United States in 1866 primarily because of dissatisfaction with the operation of the reciprocity provisions and the co-operation of British subjects with the Confederacy, American vessels were permitted to continue their navigation of the river.[26]

An agreement guaranteeing the perpetual navigation of the river was finally incorporated in the Treaty of Washington (1871). It provided that American citizens would "forever" have the "privilege" of free and open navigation of the river above the 45th parallel, both ascending and descending to the ocean, for the purpose of commerce, subject to any laws or regulations of either Great Britain or the Dominion not inconsistent with such a privilege.[27] This privilege is, of course, presently enjoyed by United States citizens.

It is significant that this treaty permits United States citizens to use the river in its natural state. There is no mention of the use of the canals in the Canadian section.[28]

Canals. Although the right to navigate the individual lakes and rivers in their natural state is important, navigation of the entire

25. 10 *Stat.* 1089, Art. IV.
26. U. S., Congress, House, *Trade with the British Provinces,* 40th Cong., 2d Sess., 1868, Ex. Doc. 240, p. 10.
27. Art. XXVI; see Appendix B. In contrast to the provision of the 1854 treaty, the privilege of navigation is available to American citizens only. This article also contains a similar provision granting Canadians perpetual navigation of the Yukon, Stikine, and Porcupine rivers in Alaska. Despite the reciprocal concession to Canada in navigating the Alaskan rivers, Sir John A. Macdonald, the Canadian Prime Minister, concluded that the British government believed that the United States had a right under international law to navigate the entire length of the river. See Pope, *op. cit.,* II, 128.
28. This matter will be discussed below. For an examination of this point, see H. J. Lawford, "Treaties and Rights of Transit on the St. Lawrence," *Canadian Bar Review,* XXXIX (1961), 577–602.

Great Lakes system is impossible without access to the connecting canals and locks. This applies not only to ocean-going vessels that utilize the St. Lawrence Seaway but also to lakers that traverse the lakes. The most widely known of these canals are the Welland Ship Canal constructed in Canada to bypass the Niagara Falls, the St. Lawrence Seaway constructed in the international section of the river to permit the entrance of ocean-going vessels, and the Sault Ste Marie Canals in the St. Mary's River connecting Lakes Huron and Superior.

The first treaty provisions relative to the use of the canals were incorporated in the Reciprocity Treaty (1854). American citizens and inhabitants obtained national treatment privileges in the use of the Canadian canals in traveling from the Great Lakes to the ocean. This privilege was conditional, however, with the British government possessing a right to suspend the privilege. For its part, the United States agreed to urge the respective state governments to allow British subjects to use their canals on terms of equality with the inhabitants of the United States.[29] Although treaty access to the canals was terminated with the abrogation of the treaty in 1866, the Canadian government permitted American vessels to continue to use the Canadian canals, and the St. Mary's Falls Canal remained open to Canadian vessels.[30]

Because of the abrogation of the Reciprocity Treaty, provisions concerning the use of canals along the Great Lakes were incorporated in the Treaty of Washington. In that treaty American citizens did not obtain a guaranteed right to use the Canadian canals, but merely an assurance from the British government that it would urge the Dominion government to accord to American citizens national treatment in the use of the Canadian canals. The United States government did, however, guarantee to British subjects national treatment in the use of the St. Clair Flats canal (since this canal was under the control of the federal government, such a guarantee could be given). In addition it agreed a second

---

29. 10 *Stat.* 1089, Art. IV.
30. Subsequently the Canadian government argued that none of the state canals had been open to Canadian vessels in the period 1854–1866. See *For. Rel.* (1892), p. 328. See, however, Charles Moore, ed. and comp., *The St. Mary's Falls Canal* (Detroit: Published by the Semi-Centennial Commission, 1907), pp. 159–160.

time to urge the states to accord to British subjects national treatment in the use of the state canals connected with the navigation of the lakes or rivers traversed by or contiguous to the boundary line.[31]

A more specific guarantee of the use of the canals is incorporated in the 1909 Boundary Waters Treaty. So long as that treaty remains in force, navigation of all canals connecting boundary waters that are in use or that may be constructed on either side of the line is guaranteed on a national treatment basis to the inhabitants and vessels of the United States and Canada.[32] It is significant that this provision applies only to the canals connecting the boundary waters. Thus it does not encompass the canals located in the Canadian section of the St. Lawrence River. It has been mentioned that Article XXVI of the Treaty of Washington relating to American navigation of the Canadian section of the St. Lawrence River does not contain any provision regarding the use of the Canadian canals. Accordingly United States citizens and vessels do not possess a treaty right to use these Canadian canals.

It is also important to note that this treaty provision does not apply to naval vessels. Such vessels must obtain special permission from the territorial government to use the canals.[33]

Comprehensive provisions regarding the use of the canals were incorporated in the unperfected 1932 St. Lawrence Waterway Treaty and the 1941 exchange of notes on the same subject. Both

31. 18 *Stat.* 355, Art. XXVII. The change in the wording relative to the Canadian canals was the result of the protests of Sir John A. Macdonald, who asserted that England had no more right to grant transit through the Canadian canals than it had to grant the French free transit over the London and Northwestern Railroads. See Pope, *op. cit.*, II, 104, 128. On November 29, 1871, President Grant sent letters to the governors of New York, Indiana, Illinois, Michigan, Ohio, Pennsylvania, and Wisconsin urging that they allow British subjects to use the canals under their jurisdiction. *For. Rel.* (1875), p. 531.

32. Art. I. Under the present treaty, use of the canals is permitted to inhabitants and vessels of the United States and Canada. In 1854 the privilege extended to British subjects and citizens and inhabitants of the United States. In 1871 the privilege was available only to citizens and subjects.

33. See the statement of Secretary of State Elihu Root before the Senate Committee on Foreign Relations. U. S., Congress, Senate, Committee on Foreign Relations, *Hearings and Proceedings on Treaty between United States and Canada Concerning Boundary Waters*, 61st Cong., 2d Sess., 1910, p. 3; and letters in Governor General file R.G. 7, G. 21, No. 192 E (Public Archives of Canada). Generally the U. S. used the canals to send vessels to the lakes for training purposes.

instruments provided that the citizens of either party had the right to use the canals of the Great Lakes and the St. Lawrence River then in existence or constructed in the future. This provision would have opened all canals on the entire Great Lakes—St. Lawrence system.[34]

One of the most significant developments relative to the navigation of the Great Lakes system was the construction of the St. Lawrence Seaway and its opening in 1959. The seaway, which provides a minimum channel of twenty-seven feet, makes it possible for ocean-going vessels to navigate the entire 2,300 mile waterway into the heart of North America.[35] Both the United States and Canada undertook certain construction projects. In addition the United States undertook navigational improvements in the Detroit River, the St. Clair River, and the St. Mary's River.[36]

Unlike the 1932 treaty and the 1941 exchange of notes, both of which contained specific provisions regarding the use of the new canals, the 1954 exchange of notes that sets forth joint co-operation on the seaway project does not contain any specific provision guaranteeing the unimpeded use of all the canals. The Canadian government desired a specific treaty arrangement guaranteeing navigation rights through the canals, but the American negotia-

34. See Art. VII in Appendix H. See also For. Rel. (1941), III, 149–168. Both instruments also provided that the rights of navigation accorded under existing treaties would be maintained notwithstanding any provision for termination included in the treaties. The intent of this provision was to elevate to a perpetual right navigation on the entire Great Lakes—St. Lawrence system. See the statement by James Grafton Rogers, Assistant Secretary of State, in U. S., Congress, Senate, Subcommittee of the Committee on Foreign Relations, Hearings on the St. Lawrence Waterway, 72d Cong., 2d Sess., 1932, p. 294.

35. There are numerous studies that relate to the legal framework of the seaway and the politics of its approval. For a comprehensive and valuable study, see William R. Willoughby, The St. Lawrence Waterway (Madison: University of Wisconsin Press, 1961). Legal materials are found in Whiteman, Digest, III, 908–918; and in Maxwell Cohen and Gilbert Nadeau, "The Legal Framework of the St. Lawrence Seaway," in Paul O. Proehl, ed., Legal Problems of International Trade (Urbana: University of Illinois Press, 1959), pp. 29–50.

36. Projects assigned to the United States included the construction of a ten-mile Long Sault canal with two locks near Massena, New York; a three-mile Point Rockway canal; and the enlargement of channels near Cornwall Island. Canada constructed four locks in the Canadian section of the river between Montreal and Cornwall; a ten-mile canal along the south shore opposite Montreal; and deepened the channels between the locks of the Welland Canal. See also 70 Stat. 54. Since most of the improvements involved operations on the Canadian side of the boundary, exchange of notes was entered into by the parties. See T.I.A.S. nos. 3772, 3814, and 4199.

tors doubted their ability to enter into such a treaty arrangement that might circumscribe Congress' legislative powers.[37] Accordingly there is in the exchange of notes only a weak reference to the right of navigation. The two governments agree that they will avoid placing any unreasonable restrictions on the transit of passengers, shipping, or trade through the international section of the seaway. Moreover they will consult together before either party promulgates any law relative to the national parts of the seaway that might affect either Canadian, American, or third-party shipping proceeding to or from either riparian country.[38]

Since the seaway must generate a sufficient amount of revenue to amortize the construction costs within fifty years, the toll charges and the division of revenue have been determined by agreement between the two parties. The division allocates 71 per cent of the revenue to Canada and 29 per cent to the United States.[39] Although the toll charges were to be reviewed by the governments in 1964, the review has been postponed for an additional two years.[40] Tolls for the use of the national canals and locks are set by the respective governments, the only requirement being that they be applied equally and without discrimination to the citizens and vessels of both states.[41] Acting within its authority, the Canadian government has recently suspended toll charges for the use of the Welland Canal.[42]

The bilateral treaties discussed above that guarantee the navigation of the Great Lakes system must be considered in the light

37. Willoughby, *op. cit.,* p. 262.
38. Exchange of Notes, Aug. 17, 1954, 5 U.S.T. 1784.
39. For the agreement on the tariff of tolls, March 9, 1959, see T.I.A.S. 4192.
40. See agreement of June 30, 1964, T.I.A.S. 5608.
41. This is required by Art. I of the Boundary Waters Treaty.
   In the 1890's a dispute developed between the United States and Canada over the latter's practice of granting rebates on the tolls for the use of the Welland Canal for grain being shipped to Montreal and setting lower tolls for coal being carried eastbound through the canal, generally in Canadian vessels. Vessels carrying coal westbound paid a higher toll (such vessels were generally American). Although the Treaty of Washington did not contain any specific provision regarding the establishment of tolls for the canals, the United States government took the position that the Canadian practice discriminated against American vessels, ports, consumers, and trade routes and in retaliation imposed a toll on all cargo passing through the St. Mary's Falls Canal destined for a Canadian port. Subsequently the rebate system and the retaliatory toll were abolished. See *For. Rel.* (1892), pp. 250 ff.; and 27 *Stat.* 267.
42. See 13 U.S.T. 1763; and 15 U.S.T. 271.

of Article 103 of the United Nations Charter. That article provides that in the event of a conflict between a member state's obligations under the Charter and those under any other international agreement, the Charter obligations shall prevail. This provision, of course, applies to other treaties between the United States and Canada, but it may be more appropriate in the case of navigation on the Great Lakes and St. Lawrence River. Without accepting the likelihood of such an event, one can postulate a situation in which the Security Council might call upon either the United States or Canada to deny the use of the Great Lakes and the seaway to the other in order to carry out the decisions of the Security Council.[43] Such a requirement would place a very difficult burden upon the co-riparian state. In this regard Richard R. Baxter states that the riparian state should not be expected to carry the whole burden of collective security. Until an effective form of collective security is established, the co-riparian state should not be required to assume a greater share of the responsibility for fulfilling decisions of the Security Council than other states.[44]

Navigation Rights of Third States

Since the waters of the Great Lakes and the St. Lawrence River are national and not international, vessels of third-party states have no legal right of navigation without the permission of the riparian states. The treaties guaranteeing the free and open navigation of the lakes and rivers referred to above apply only to the vessels of the United States and Canada.

Both the United States and Canada are parties to numerous commercial treaties that accord to various states the right to enter their respective ports and waters for the purpose of commerce.[45]

43. Similar concern was expressed in 1926 as a result of British and Canadian membership in the League of Nations. See the confidential memorandum of the Judge Advocate General, U. S. Army, in Department of State file 711.42157 Sa 29/260 (National Archives).

44. Richard R. Baxter, *The Law of International Waterways* (Cambridge: Harvard University Press, 1964), pp. 238–239.

45. For a discussion of these treaties, see Don C. Piper, "Navigation Provisions in United States Commercial Treaties," *American Journal of Comparative Law*, XI

The standard of treatment accorded by such treaties is generally most-favored-nation treatment, national treatment, or both. With regard to United States commercial treaties, it is clearly understood that the right of entry into American ports includes the ports along the Great Lakes. Even in the absence of a treaty provision, the United States as a matter of public policy permits freedom of navigation on the Great Lakes by commercial vessels of all friendly nations in time of peace.[46] These bilateral treaties do not, of course, contain any provision relating to transit through the waters of the co-riparian state. Since it is physically impossible to proceed to the ports of the Great Lakes without passing through the territory of both riparian states, the privileges accorded to third states by treaty or public policy are significant.

In this regard we must note that there is no specific understanding between the United States and Canada whereby one party agrees to permit vessels of a third party to navigate its waters in order to call at the Great Lakes—St. Lawrence ports of the other party. There is in other words no bilateral agreement between the two that precludes Canada's closing the St. Lawrence River to the vessels of a third state that intend to call at Chicago or Detroit or the United States' closing its waters to those bound for Canadian ports.

As a matter of policy it is quite unlikely that either riparian state would take any action to exclude all third-party vessels from the Great Lakes and St. Lawrence. To do so would certainly defeat the purpose of the St. Lawrence Seaway. However, it is not inconceivable that one state for reasons of public policy might exclude vessels from a particular state. This possibility is considered in the exchange of notes relative to the St. Lawrence Seaway, but it is not effectively resolved. The governments agree to consult with one another before promulgating any laws or regulations applicable to the national sections of the seaway that might affect third-party shipping proceeding to or from either party.[47]

(1962), 184–204; and H. J. Lawford, "Treaties and Rights of Transit on the St. Lawrence," *Canadian Bar Review*, XXXIX (1961), 577–602.

46. Whiteman, *Digest*, III, 917.

47. Exchange of Notes, Aug. 17, 1954, 5 U.S.T. 1704.

The requirement of consultation does not, however, bar action by either party. The problem is essentially one of balancing the recognized right of the territorial sovereign to control the entry of foreign vessels into its territory and the practical necessity to co-operate fully in order to obtain the optimum benefit from the joint projects.

A bar to unilateral action is set forth in Article V of the General Agreement on Tariffs and Trade to which both the United States and Canada are parties. That article sets forth the freedom of transit through the territories of the member states for traffic in transit to or from the territory of other contracting parties.[48] Accordingly neither riparian state may exclude vessels from a third state carrying goods from one contracting party to the other riparian state. Although this article does limit the freedom of either riparian state to exclude third-party vessels from the Great Lakes—St. Lawrence system, it does not mean that all third-party vessels must be permitted freedom of transit. The right applies only to those carrying cargo from one contracting party to either riparian state.

Navigation Practices on the Great Lakes

The legal right to navigate the Great Lakes is supplemented by several treaties and agreements that establish the rules and procedures for the effective and safe navigation of the Great Lakes—St. Lawrence system. These arrangements are of two types: those that relate specifically to privileges and benefits accorded to Canadian and American vessels, and those that initially related only to lakers but with the opening of the seaway apply to all vessels. Generally the rules and practices are unique to the lakes, although in some instances they are modifications of rules appli-

---

48. See 61 *Stat.* (5) (6). Art. V reads *inter alia:* ". . . there shall be freedom of transit through the territory of each contracting party, via the routes most convenient for international transit, for traffic in transit to or from the territory of other contracting parties. No distinction shall be made which is based on the flag of vessels, the place of origin, departure, entry, exit or destination, or on any circumstances relating to the ownership of goods, of vessels or of other means of transport."

cable to the high seas. In this regard it should be noted that general international conventions that relate to the high seas do not relate to the Great Lakes.

Coasting trade. Both the United States and Canada as a matter of policy restrict participation in the Great Lakes—St. Lawrence coasting trade to their respective national vessels. Under United States law vessels participating in the coasting trade must be built in the United States, owned by United States citizens, and documented under the laws of the United States.[49] In addition United States commercial treaties customarily contain a provision that specifically reserves participation in the coasting trade to national vessels. In a few of the treaties foreign vessels are accorded most-favored-nation treatment with regard to the coasting trade.[50] Until 1961 the Canadian coasting trade was open to British vessels under the terms of the 1931 Commonwealth Merchant Shipping Agreement. In that year, however, the Canadian government instituted measures to restrict participation in the Great Lakes—St. Lawrence coasting trade to Canadian vessels.[51] Like the United States, Canada has not accorded in its commercial treaties national treatment with regard to the coasting trade.[52]

Notwithstanding their restrictive policy, both the United States and Canada have made temporary exceptions in favor of the other. Because of temporary shortages of American lakers, Canadian vessels have been permitted to transport coal from American lake ports to Ogdensburg, New York, and to carry grain and iron ore between American ports. These privileges (authorized by Congress) were extended for specified periods of time and are no longer in force. In addition, Canadian vessels are presently permitted to carry passengers from Rochester to Alexandria Bay,

49. 46 U.S.C. secs. 289, 883.
50. Piper, *American Journal of Comparative Law*, XI, 193–196.
51. Canada, House of Commons, *Parliamentary Debates*, 1961, pp. 4712, 5218. See Canada, *Statutes at Large*, 9–10 Eliz. II, c. 32. The Royal Commission on Coasting Trade recommended against restricting the coasting trade to Canadian vessels. See *Report of the Royal Commission on Coasting Trade* (Ottawa: Queen's Printer, 1958), p. 139.
52. See the statement of H. C. Kingstone, from the legal division, Department of External Affairs, in Canada, Senate, *Proceedings of the Standing Committee on Transport and Communications* (1959), p. 116.

New York. This privilege was initially granted in 1936 and is to remain in force until an American company establishes a passenger service between the two ports.[53]

With the opening of the seaway, exceptions in favor of Canadian vessels may no longer be possible without involving vessels of third states. Those states that enjoy a most-favored-nation provision with regard to the coasting trade would be entitled to share in any benefits accorded to Canadian vessels.

Near the turn of the century and in the 1920's American vessels were also permitted on an informal basis to carry grain between Canadian ports when Canadian lake tonnage was insufficient to transport the grain from the western to the eastern ports. Permission to carry the grain was usually granted toward the close of the navigation season and was generally for one voyage per vessel. In such instances there was no formal amendment in the coasting laws but a waiver of the penalties against foreign participation.[54]

For a brief period in the 1870's and 1880's, British and American vessels were allowed to participate in the coasting trade under treaty auspices. This privilege, incorporated into the Treaty of Washington, allowed vessels of either party to carry goods without the payment of a duty between the North American ports of the other provided a portion of the transportation was made through the territory of the first party by land carriage and in bond. The privilege was subsequently renounced by the United States after a ten-year period.[55]

Since that time occasional suggestions have been made that the two governments conclude a treaty permitting reciprocal partici-

53. 46 U.S.C. sec. 883. Permission for Canadian vessels to carry coal was granted for 1956–1957, 70 *Stat.* 1090; for iron ore from 1941 to 1952, 66 *Stat.* 156; and for grain during 1951 only, 65 *Stat.* 371. See also 46 U.S.C. sec. 289a. In a recent case, *United States* v. *1500 Cords, More or Less, Jackpipe Pulpwood*, 108 F. Supp. 224 (1952), the court held that a Canadian tug sweeping pulpwood logs floating in the Minnesota Bay of Lake Superior into the towing booms of an American steamer performed no part of the transportation of the log raft between American ports in violation of the coasting regulations.
54. See Department of State file 842.801 (National Archives); and Laurier papers, numbers 8730, 38147, 38184, 39245 (Public Archives of Canada). In 1923 a Royal Commission recommended that American vessels be permitted to carry grain for winter storage in order to make shipping rates competitive. See Canada, *Sessional Paper*, No. 221 (1923), pp. 51–53; and G. P. de T. Glazebrook, *A History of Transportation in Canada* (Toronto: Ryerson Press, 1938), p. 425.
55. 18 *Stat.* 355, Art. XXX. See also *For. Rel.* (1883), p. 414.

pation in the coasting trade or the carrying of goods for export between the ports of the other. Although negotiations were undertaken in some instances, the parties were not able to agree upon a treaty.[56]

In a related matter, suggestions have recently been made by the shipping industry in both countries that the two governments conclude a treaty restricting the transboundary trade to vessels of either party. It is argued that unless this is done the lake shipping industry will lose much of its business to ocean-going vessels that can operate at a lower cost.[57] Neither government has shown any support for such an arrangement, which, in view of the existing commercial treaties to which both governments are parties, might be difficult to accomplish.

Double taxation. Another bilateral arrangement that benefits directly United States and Canadian shipping interests and facilitates the optimum use of the Great Lakes as an artery of waterborne transportation is the double taxation agreement of 1928. Under this agreement, United States citizens not resident in Canada are exempt from Canadian income tax on earnings from sources within Canada derived from the operation of American ships in Canadian waters. In like fashion persons resident in Canada not citizens of the United States are exempt from United States income tax on the earnings from sources within the United States derived from the operation of Canadian ships in United States waters.[58] Although this agreement does not specifically refer to the Great Lakes—St. Lawrence, it provides substantial benefits to steamship lines operating in that area.

56. The unperfected Brown-Fish treaty of 1874 contained a provision for reciprocal participation in the coasting trade. See Department of State file, Unperfected M-11 (National Archives). Similar suggestions were made in 1906 and 1934. See Governor General file R.G. 7, G. 21, No. 301, Vol. 3(a) (Public Archives of Canada); and *For. Rel.* (1935), II, 35–53.

57. See *Submission of Dominion Marine Association to the Royal Commission on Coasting Trade* (1955), and the Commission's *Report* (cited in n. 51, *supra*), at p. 139. A congressional resolution on the same subject died in committee. See U. S., *Congressional Record*, 83d Cong., 2d Sess., C, Part I, 60.

58. Exchange of Notes for Relief from Double Income Tax on Shipping Profits, Aug. 2 and Sept. 17, 1928. 47 *Stat.* 2580. It should be noted that the exemption benefits United States citizens in Canada, and in the U. S. "persons resident in Canada." This latter phrase would appear to include both citizens and aliens.

Salvage and wrecking. The reciprocal right to render salvage and wrecking services to vessels disabled on the waters and shores of the contiguous lakes and rivers of the Great Lakes—St. Lawrence system (excluding Lake Michigan and the Welland Canal) without reference to the international boundary is guaranteed by the treaty of 1908.[59] This treaty incorporates the privileges that had been reciprocally granted in the 1890's by municipal legislation.[60] Although neither the treaty nor the statute specifically permit Canadian salvage operations in Lake Michigan, neither instrument specifically prohibits such operations. This has raised the question whether Canadian salvage vessels should be allowed to operate on Lake Michigan. The federal government's position appears to be that so long as American salvage vessels are available, Canadian vessels will be limited to the waters specified in the treaty.[61]

Safety by means of radio. In an effort to promote the safety of life and property on the Great Lakes, the United States and Canada have concluded an agreement requiring that all merchant vessels of five hundred gross tons and over and all passenger vessels of sixty-five feet or more be equipped with a radio-telephone installation. The applicable waters for the agreement include all of the lakes, the connecting and tributary waters, and the St. Lawrence River as far east as Montreal, but exclude the Niagara River and the tributary waters which are not connecting waters. Vessels subject to the agreement are required to have a crew member qualified to operate the installation so that there may be "continuous effective listening" on the distress frequency.

Third-party vessels that navigate the Great Lakes are also subject to the requirements with the riparian governments assisting them to meet the standards of the agreement to the extent permitted by their constitutional procedures. Each party may ex-

59. 35 *Stat.* 2035, Art. II. See Appendix D.
60. 46 U.S.C. secs. 316, 725. Canada, *Rev. Stat.* (1952), c. 276. See also *For. Rel.* (1892), pp. 290–295.
61. See Department of State file 711.42/124, 125; and 711.429 Salvage and Wreckage Rights/8 (National Archives).

empt certain of its own or third-party vessels from the requirements if circumstances warrant such exemption.[62]

Quarantine inspection. In order to facilitate the arrival of vessels from foreign ports at the Great Lakes, the United States and
Canada have agreed that such vessels will be inspected by the
authorities of the government having jurisdiction over the primary port of arrival. Following the initial inspection, the vessels
are given a free *pratique* that is accepted by the authorities of the
other party without the necessity of a reinspection.[63]

This agreement was concluded under the aegis of Articles LVI
and LVII of the International Sanitary Convention, 1926, by
which governments might enter into special agreements in order
to make the sanitary provisions more efficacious and less burden-
some.[64]

In this same matter, United States law provides that vessels
plying between foreign ports near its frontiers do not require a
bill of health before departing from the foreign port. Although
the Canadian lake ports are not specifically mentioned in the
Code, they apparently are within the scope of the law.[65]

Load line regulations. Because the buoyancy of saline water is
greater than that of fresh water, load line computations for ocean-
going vessels are different from those for lake vessels. Recognizing this fact, the International Load Line Convention, 1930,
exempts vessels engaged solely on the Great Lakes from the requirements of the convention. Consequently both the United
States and Canada have promulgated special load line regulations
which are applicable to all passenger or cargo vessels of one
hundred fifty gross tons plying the waters of the Great Lakes.[66] To

62. Agreement for the Promotion of Safety on the Great Lakes by Means of
Radio, Feb. 21, 1952, T.I.A.S. 2666. See also 68 *Stat.* 729; 47 U.S.C. sec. 352, 507;
Canada, *Statutes at Large*, 1–2 Eliz. II, c. 20; P.C. 1954–1924, Dec. 8, 1954,
Canada, *SOR Consolidation* (1955), p. 445; P.C. 1954–1681, Nov. 3, 1954, in
ibid., p. 301; and U. S., Congress, House, *Safety on the Great Lakes by Means of
Radio*, 83d Cong., 2d Sess., 1954, Rept. 2284.
63. Exchange of notes, Oct. 10 and 23, 1929. 47 *Stat.* 2573.
64. 45 *Stat.* 2494.
65. 42 U.S.C. sec. 269(d).
66. Henry Reiff, *The United States and the Treaty Law of the Sea* (Minneapolis: University of Minnesota Press, 1959), p. 143. See the Final Protocol of the

facilitate commerce on the lakes, each has granted reciprocal recognition to the other's load line regulations for vessels engaged in international voyages on the Great Lakes.[67]

Rules of the road. Establishment of common rules of the road for the Great Lakes was an indispensible requirement for the optimum use of the waterway for commercial purposes. The rules have as their basic foundation the international rules of the road modified to take into account the unique characteristics of the lakes and inland navigation.[68] Although both the United States and Canada are parties to the multilateral international conventions and regulations relative to the international rules of the road, they have not concluded any bilateral agreement relative to the rules of the road for the Great Lakes. Each federal state promulgates rules within its jurisdiction. Uniformity in the rules has been achieved by the process of discussion and negotiation with the enactment of concurrent legislation. The navigational rules encompass the Great Lakes and the connecting and tributary waters including the St. Lawrence River as far east as Montreal, and apply to all vessels regardless of nationality.[69]

Until 1895 the international rules applied to the Great Lakes as

---

Convention, July 5, 1930, 47 *Stat.* 2228. See also 46 U.S.C. sec. 88; Canada, *Rev. Stat.* (1952), c. 29, sec. 429; P.C. 1954–1926, Dec. 8, 1954, in Canada, *SOR Consolidation* (1955), p. 471.

67. In 1935 Congress passed the Coastwise Load Line Act, 1935, 49 *Stat.* 891, which authorized the reciprocal recognition of foreign load line regulations when the proper authorities were satisfied that they met the American standards. See the exchange of notes, 1938–1940, 54 *Stat.* 2300.

68. For the text of the Canadian rules, see P.C. 1954–1927, Dec. 8, 1954, in Canada, *SOR Consolidation* (1955), pp. 501–515; for the text of the American rules see 33 U.S.C. secs. 241–295; and U. S., Coast Guard, *Rules of the Road: Great Lakes* (Washington: Government Printing Office, 1959). See also 72 *Stat.* 49. See also *The Kindoc v. Canadian Steamship Lines, Ltd.,* [1931] S.C.R. 228, where the Canadian Supreme Court declared that the Great Lakes rules of the road were valid as far east as the lower exit of the Lachine Canal and the Victoria Bridge at Montreal.

When the navigation regulations prescribed by Congress do not specifically apply to a situation, resort is had to the general principles of navigation which may be deduced from decisions of admiralty courts. Such rules are applicable except insofar as they are inconsistent with existing statutes. See *The George W. Roby,* 111 F. 601, 609 (1901).

69. Until 1958 the U. S. navigation rules applied only to U. S. vessels on the Great Lakes. In that year the rules were amended to encompass all vessels in U. S. waters of the Great Lakes. 72 *Stat.* 49. See Whiteman, *Digest,* III, 753–754 for statement by Legal Adviser Hackworth that Art. I of the Boundary Waters Treaty did not serve to extend the navigation rules to Canadian vessels in U. S. waters.

well as the high seas. In that year the United States enacted special rules for the lakes, which the Canadian government was not then willing to accept.[70] In 1905 that government finally proclaimed special rules for the lakes which differed in some respects from the United States rules. These were gradually amended following consultation with American authorities and in 1916 they were made identical with the United States rules.[71] The uniqueness of lake navigation is still recognized today with reference to navigational rules. The International Convention for the Safety of Life at Sea, 1948, which contains provisions relative to construction, life-saving appliances, radio-telegraphy, safety of navigation, and certificates, provides that the regulations shall not apply to vessels navigating solely the Great Lakes and their connecting and tributary waters. In addition the International Regulations for Preventing Collisions at Sea, 1948, provides that there may be special rules relative to inland navigation.[72]

Pilotage requirements. Another example of mutual co-operation concerning navigational matters is the recent establishment of pilotage requirements for the Great Lakes. The United States initiated action in this matter with the enactment of the Great Lakes Pilotage Act, 1960, which makes mandatory the use of pilots by ocean-going vessels in certain designated United States waters.[73] The Canadian Parliament subsequently enacted similar

70. In 1895 new international rules were to be implemented which the Attorney General ruled would be applicable to the Great Lakes since they were regarded as high seas. The special rules were then adopted to meet the specific requirements of the lakes. Act of Feb. 8, 1895, 28 *Stat.* 645; U. S., Congress, House, *Navigation on the Great Lakes*, 52d Cong., 3d Sess., 1895, Rept. 1682. See also 21 *Ops. Atty. Gen.* 106. In giving his opinion the Attorney General referred to *United States* v. *Rodgers*, 150 U. S. 249 (1893), where the Supreme Court declared that for purposes of criminal jurisdiction the Great Lakes would be regarded as high seas.

71. In 1914 Canada suggested the establishment of a joint committee to decide upon a set of rules to be adopted by both parties. Because of the war, the committee was held in abeyance and in 1916 Canada amended its rules to make them identical to those of the United States. See Department of State file 711.42156/1, 3, 6, 12 (National Archives); and Governor General file R.G. 7, G. 21, No. 257, Vol. 1(a) (Public Archives of Canada).

72. T.I.A.S. 2495, Regulations, c. I, Reg. 3(b); T.I.A.S. 2899, rule 30.

73. P.L. 86–555, June 30, 1960, 74 *Stat.* 259. For background material see U. S., Congress, Senate, *Pilotage Requirements for Vessels Navigating the U. S. Waters of the Great Lakes*, 86th Cong., 2d Sess., 1960, Rept. 1284; *idem*, Merchant Marine and Fisheries Subcommittee of the Committee on Interstate and Foreign Commerce, *Hearings, Great Lakes Pilotage*, 86th Cong., 2d Sess., 1960; and *idem*, House, *Providing for Certain Pilotage Requirements in the Navigation of U. S. Waters of the Great Lakes*, 86th Cong., 2d Sess., 1960, Rept. 1666. This was not

legislation designating Canadian waters where the use of pilots is mandatory.[74] Both the President and the Governor General in Council have designated similar areas where all ocean-going vessels must employ either an American or Canadian pilot.[75] In the open waters of the lakes, not designated as requiring the use of a pilot, there must be a pilot on board or an officer qualified to direct the navigation of the vessel in the undesignated areas. Such an officer is one who has been designated by either government as competent to navigate the lakes. Canadian and American lakers are exempted from the provisions of the acts on a reciprocal basis. In addition American lakers do not pay pilotage dues on the St. Lawrence above Montreal.[76] In like manner Canadian pilots may be used in American waters so long as Canada extends reciprocal privileges to American pilots. In this regard the Secretary of Commerce and the Minister of Transport have entered into several agreements for the equitable utilization of Canadian and American pilots and the establishment of joint rates for pilotage services.[77]

•   •   •   •   •

Viewing the pattern of legal developments relating to the Great Lakes, one can immediately see that the primary concern of the nineteenth century was the development of an effective legal regime for navigation. These problems were, however, largely resolved by 1871, with Article I of the 1909 treaty being essentially a reaffirmation of existing rights. The primary concern in the twentieth century is not in promoting navigation but in developing an effective legal regime relating to the non-navigable use of the waters of the Great Lakes—St. Lawrence.

---

the first discussion of compulsory pilotage services. In the 1930's a draft treaty regarding use of pilots on the Great Lakes was prepared. See Department of State file 711.42156 Pilotage/1, 35, 40, 45 (National Archives).

74. Canada, *Statutes at Large*, 8–9 Eliz. II, c. 40.

75. 12 U.S.T. 1033. The initial draft of U. S. legislation had required the use of pilots throughout all American lake waters. When the Canadian and other governments protested, the legislation was amended to provide for designated areas. See hearings cited in note 73, pp. 5–10. As enacted the statute provides that the President in designating pilotage areas shall give due regard to the "foreign relations of the United States."

76. Canada, *Statutes at Large*, 9–10 Eliz. II, c. 32.

77. See 12 U.S.T. 1033; 14 U.S.T. 226; and 14 U.S.T. 1627. The agreements by the Secretary of Commerce must receive the concurrence of the Secretary of State.

· 6 ·

Use and Control of Water Resources

It has been mentioned that in the twentieth century the primary concern of the United States and Canada with regard to the Great Lakes has been the development of an effective legal regime to facilitate the optimum utilization of the lakes for non-navigation purposes. The development of such a regime must of course take into account the previously existing navigation regime with its established treaty rights. Because the Great Lakes—St. Lawrence is one watershed, international co-operation is as essential for the non-navigable use of the lakes as it is for their navigable use. In this regard the riparian states have not been able to look to accepted general principles of international law relating to the non-navigable use of flowing water, for this is a new field of international law and many of the general principles are propositions laid down *de lege ferenda*.[1] Rather they have looked to treaty law and the bilateral formulation of basic principles governing the use of the common water resources. They have been in the forefront in the establishment of such treaty rules. These rules have been tailored to fulfil the requirements of the Great Lakes and do not necessarily meet the needs of other international waterways. The basic purpose of the rules is, however, universal: to develop the entire system for the optimum benefit of the regional community notwithstanding the division of political sovereignty.

The discussion will relate to the international machinery and legal principles for the control of the waterway, the work of the

1. See United Nations, Economic Commission for Europe, Committee on Electric Power, *Legal Aspects of the Hydro-Electric Development of Rivers and Lakes of Common Interest* (E/ECE/136) (Geneva, 1952), p. 38.

International Joint Commission, and some of the problems that have emerged relating to water utilization.

International Machinery and Governing Principles

The establishment of international machinery and the formulation of general legal principles to govern the utilization of the Great Lakes—St. Lawrence waterway have been simultaneous developments. The initial machinery was the International Waterways Commission, which participated in the formulation of the legal principles. The present machinery, the International Joint Commission, and agreed legal principles are set forth in the Boundary Waters Treaty.

The International Waterways Commission. The first formal attempt to consider boundary waters problems on a broad scale occurred in 1902 when Congress authorized the President to invite the British government to participate in the establishment of an international waterways commission to investigate and report on the conditions and uses of the waters adjacent to the Canadian—United States boundary. Matters to be considered by the commission included such problems as water levels, the effect and regulation of water diversion, and recommendations for the improvement of navigation.[2] The proposed commission met with eager approval in Canada, but its establishment was delayed for several years because of different interpretations of the commission's authority. The State Department interpreted the congressional authorization to encompass only the waters of the Great Lakes and the rivers which had their natural outlet to the ocean via the St. Lawrence River. The Canadian government was anx-

2. 32 *Stat.* 372. It was suggested in 1895 that the United States, Canada, and Mexico establish a commission to adjudicate the rights on the international streams of North America. See U. S., Congress, Senate, *Address to the People of the United States by the National Irrigation Congress, Fourth Annual Session, at Albuquerque, New Mexico, September 16–19, 1895,* 54th Cong., 1st Sess., 1896, Doc. 253; and C. J. Chacko, *The International Joint Commission between the United States of America and the Dominion of Canada* (New York: Columbia University Press, 1932), pp. 72–73.

ious to have the obstructions in the St. John River investigated by a joint commission and urged that the commission encompass all waters adjacent to the international boundary. The former interpretation prevailed, however; the Commission was finally established in 1905.[3]

During its eight-year existence the Commission investigated and reported on such matters as the Chicago diversion, the Niagara Falls, and the use of the waters at Sault Ste Marie, and also delineated the international boundary through the St. Lawrence River and the Great Lakes.[4] As part of its technical studies the Commission had occasion to consider the formulation of general principles that would relate to the use and diversion of the boundary waters and all streams that flowed across the boundary. The Canadian members proposed that the Commission prepare for the benefit of both governments legal principles concerning the waterway. In addition they recommended that a permanent joint commission be established to deal more effectively and satisfactorily with all disputes concerning the specific application of the proposed general principles. The proposal was not accepted by the United States members, who considered that the enunciation of general principles was beyond the scope of their authority.[5] Despite their inability to agree upon the enunciation of general principles, the Commissioners did agree that in the absence of a governing treaty provision, the territorial sovereign could rightfully use and divert waters within its jurisdiction for any purpose. They also agreed that international comity prescribed that in the absence of necessity a state should not exercise its power to the injury of a friendly state or its citizens without the consent of that state. Injury of the citizens of one riparian state by

3. For the exchange of notes establishing the International Waterways Commission, see "Compiled Reports of the International Waterways Commission, 1905–1913," in Canada, *Sessional Papers*, No. 19a, XLVII, No. 12 (1913), 8, 20–33. This Paper is a useful compilation of the reports, memoranda, and papers of the Commission.

4. For a brief summary of the work of the International Waterways Commission, see the "Progress Report" of the American Section (in document cited in n. 3, *supra*), pp. 1078–1103.

5. See the "Joint Report of the International Waterways Commission on the Conditions Existing at Niagara Falls, with Recommendations," (May 3, 1906) (in document cited in n. 3, *supra*), pp. 339–340.

the actions of another was a breach of international comity that entitled the injured party to retaliate.

The Commission realized that questions involving the same fundamental principles of water utilization would arise in the future and "create friction, hostile feelings and reprisals." Accordingly it recommended that the United States and Great Britain conclude a treaty stating the rules and incorporating principles by which all water problems might be peacefully and satisfactorily resolved. In this respect, it suggested the following primary uses for the boundary waters: (1) for necessary domestic and sanitary purposes, (2) for service of locks and navigation purposes, and (3) for purposes of navigation. In addition it suggested that the treaty prohibit the permanent diversion of navigable streams that cross the international boundary or that form part of the boundary, except upon an adjustment of the rights of all concerned parties by a permanent commission and with its consent.[6]

The Boundary Waters Treaty. Following the recommendations of the International Waterways Commission, the United States and Great Britain concluded the Boundary Waters Treaty (1909) to prevent disputes regarding the use of the boundary waters between the United States and Canada and to resolve all questions along the common frontier. The treaty enunciates the principles that are applicable to the boundary waters, and creates the International Joint Commission to exercise jurisdiction over the use, obstruction, or diversion of the waters.[7]

For the purposes of the treaty, boundary waters are defined as those lakes and rivers, or portions thereof, through which the international boundary passes; tributary waters are those which in their natural channels flow into such lakes or rivers (e.g., Lake

6. See the "Joint Report of the International Waterways Commission on the Application of the Minnesota Canal and Power Company for Permission to Divert Certain Waters in Minnesota" (Nov. 15, 1906) (in document cited in n. 3, *supra*), p. 368.

7. See U. S., Congress, Senate, *Legal Aspects of the Use of Systems of International Waters*, 85th Cong., 2d Sess., 1958, Doc. 118, pp. 10–62, for a history of the 1909 treaty. See especially pp. 12–15, for the text of the initial Clinton-Gibbons draft (1907). This draft was rejected by the Department of State and the task of drafting a treaty was turned over to Chandler P. Anderson.

Michigan), waters flowing from such lakes, or waters of rivers flowing across the international boundary.[8]

Principles applicable to the boundary waters and to tributary waters are set forth in the treaty and are a part of the conventional law between the United States and Canada. The principles applicable to the tributary waters are predicated on the belief that under international law a state enjoys complete jurisdiction over waters located wholly within its territory so long as its actions do not directly injure another state. Accordingly the treaty accords to each state the right to take unilateral action with regard to its tributary waters. Applicable principles are: (1) Each government reserves exclusive jurisdiction and control over use and diversion, whether temporary or permanent, of the waters. (2) Any interference with or diversion from their natural channels which results in an injury to interests on the other side of the boundary gives "rise to the same rights and entitle[s] the injured parties to the same legal remedies as if such injury took place in the country where such diversion or interference occurs. . . ." This provision does not apply, however, to cases already existing or to cases covered by special agreement. (3) Neither government surrenders any right it may have to object to any diversion or interference on the other side of the boundary that is productive of "material injury" to the navigation interests on its side of the boundary.[9]

In contrast to the principles permitting unilateral action in the tributary waters, the principles governing the boundary waters are predicated on the need for joint co-operation and set forth the procedures for the adjudication of water utilization projects by a bilateral commission, the International Joint Commission. The following principles apply to the boundary waters.

(1) In addition to those already permitted or provided for by special agreement, further or other uses, diversions, or obstructions of waters on either side of the boundary line affecting the natural flow of boundary waters on the other side of the line shall

8. Preliminary Article; see Appendix E for the text of the treaty.
9. Art. II. The first principle appears to be directly contrary to the recommendation of the International Waterways Commission.

be made only with the authority of either federal government, within its respective jurisdiction, and with the approval of the International Joint Commission. This principle is not intended, however, to interfere with the ordinary use of the waters for domestic and sanitary purposes.[10] (2) Each government may undertake works in boundary waters for the improvement of commerce and navigation provided such works are wholly on its side of the line and do not "materially affect" the flow or level of the boundary waters on the other side of the line. (3) Except in cases of special agreement, the parties will not permit the construction of any works or obstructions in the waters flowing from boundary waters or in waters at a lower level than the boundary in rivers flowing across the boundary that would raise the level of the waters on the other side without the approval of the International Joint Commission.[11] (4) Boundary waters and waters flowing across the boundary line shall not be polluted on either side to the injury of health or property on the other side of the line.[12] (5) Each party shall have equal and similar rights in the use of boundary waters on its respective side of the boundary line.[13] At the discretion of the International Joint Commission, this rule may be suspended for temporary diversions at places where an equal division of the waters cannot be advantageously made because of local conditions, and where the diversion does not diminish the amount of water available elsewhere for use on the other side.[14] (6) The following order of precedence is to be observed in the use of boundary waters and no use shall be permitted which tends "materially" to conflict with or restrain any other use which has preference over it in the order of precedence: (a) uses for domestic and sanitary purposes, (b) uses for navigation, including the service of navigation canals, and (c) uses for

10. Art. III. C. J. Chacko interprets this provision to mean that the works should not interfere with the ordinary use of such waters for domestic and sanitary purposes. His interpretation seems questionable since the treaty specifically states "such provisions" are not intended, to interfere, with an obvious intention of referring to the treaty provisions requiring the consent of the International Joint Commission for diversion or obstruction of the boundary waters. See Chacko, *op. cit.*, p. 91.
11. Art. IV.
12. Art. IV.
13. Art. VIII.
14. Art. VIII.

power and irrigation purposes. The order of precedence shall not disturb existing water uses on either side of the boundary line.[15]

The principles for the utilization and control of the boundary waters and their application by the International Joint Commission have promoted the optimum utilization of the waters with a minimum of disagreement. In contrast the principles regarding tributary waters incorporated in Article II have been challenged as being incompatible with international law and have been the subject of controversy since the negotiation of the treaty. The Canadian Prime Minister, Wilfrid Laurier, believed that the article was contrary to international law, which he was convinced did not permit the diversion of running waters. His conviction was such that he was tempted to reject the treaty but decided not to do so because of its other provisions that he considered to be very useful.[16] The leader of the opposition, Robert Borden, also took the view that the article was contrary to international law and charged that the government had entered into the treaty "with not very much regard to international law."[17]

Despite the Prime Minister's uncertainty, the Canadian negotiator, George Gibbons, insisted that the principles incorporated in Article II were a correct statement of international law, which he declared did not limit a state's right to utilize waters located wholly within its territory. In this regard he considered the Harmon doctrine to be a valid statement of international law.[18] To lessen any detrimental effect on private interests of a unilateral

15. Art. VIII. This preference is somewhat similar to that suggested by the International Waterways Commission.

16. See the letters on the treaty from Laurier to Gibbons in Gibbons Papers, Vol. 7 (Public Archives of Canada), and Canada, House of Commons, *Parliamentary Debates*, XCVIII (1910–11), 911–912.

17. *Ibid.*, pp. 872, 904–905. Borden subsequently indicated that although he criticized some of its details, he considered the treaty to be the "outstanding achievement" of Laurier's premiership. Department of State file 711.42155/621 (National Archives).

18. See letters of Gibbons to Laurier, Gibbons Papers, Vol. 8; and the memorandum on the treaty prepared by Gibbons in Gibbons Papers, Vol. 15 (Public Archives of Canada). See also Alan O. Gibbons, "Sir George Gibbons and the Boundary Waters Treaty of 1909," *Canadian Historical Review*, XXXIV (1953), 137.

See 21 *Ops. Atty. Gen.* 274 for the statement of the Harmon doctrine (Dec. 12, 1895). In this opinion Attorney General Harmon declared that the principles of international law imposed no obligation on the upper riparian to consider the interests of the lower riparian in its use of waters within its territory even though the waters flowed into another state.

diversion, Gibbons obtained a provision granting the injured parties in the co-riparian state the same legal remedies as if the injury had taken place in the country where the diversion occurred. He regarded this as a significant concession by the United States and a far-reaching step towards the protection of private rights.[19] Notwithstanding his enthusiasm, this provision has never been utilized.

Apparently one reason why the State Department favored the article was that it would protect the Chicago diversion. It is not clear however, whether the American negotiator, Chandler P. Anderson, viewed the article as an expression of the Harmon doctrine or whether he viewed it as a justified distinction between boundary waters and tributary waters.[20] The difficulty with the article is that it attempts to impose a simple legal formula upon a complex physical situation. Some waters are wholly within the territory of one or the other of the treaty parties, yet they are all part of the same watershed, and events in any one part of the watershed may affect the whole.

Whatever may have been the rationale behind the article, the provision recognizing the territorial sovereign's control over the tributary waters within its jurisdiction is part of the treaty law. The use or diversion of such waters does not require the consent of the other party. Any unilateral diversion of such waters is subject to the applicable principles of customary international law, except that neither party may assert a diplomatic claim, on behalf of private parties sustaining injury in its territory as a result of such a diversion, if compensation is available to the injured parties in the diverting country. In addition each govern-

19. See letters Gibbons to Laurier, Gibbons Papers, Vol. 8; Gibbons' comments in Papers Relating to the Work of the International Joint Commission; and letter Gibbons to Anderson, Gibbons Papers, Vol. 8 (Public Archives of Canada).

For a discussion of the possible meanings of Article II, see Robert D. Scott, "The Canadian-American Boundary Waters Treaty: Why Article II?," *The Canadian Bar Review*, XXXVI (1958), 511–547. A Canadian member of the IJC once characterized it as "unique in the history of international relations." George W. Kyte, *Organization and Work of the International Joint Commission* (Ottawa: Patenaude, 1937), p. 6. Laurier's biographer described it as "a distinctive North American contribution to a sane international polity." Oscar Douglas Skelton, *Life and Letters of Sir Wilfrid Laurier* (New York: Century, 1922), II, 363.

20. In a recent study the State Department concluded that the article was not an expression of the Harmon doctrine. See Senate, Doc. 118 (cited in n. 7, *supra*), pp. 59–60.

ment may object to any diversion or use of the tributary waters if it produces "material injury" to the navigation interests on its side of the international boundary. The right to object would not appear to be an effective legal bar to unilateral action.

The six-member International Joint Commission established by the treaty has investigatory and quasi-adjudicatory tasks. With regard to the latter, it approves all projects involving the use, obstruction, or diversion of boundary waters. In doing so it utilizes the principles mentioned above and renders decisions that are binding on the parties involved. The Commission's quasi-adjudicatory authority, as has been mentioned, does not encompass the tributary waters. At the request of either government, the Commission undertakes studies of questions or matters of difference between the two countries involving each one's rights and interests and its obligations to the other or to the inhabitants of the other along the common boundary. In this instance the Commission's reports are merely recommendations to the governments and are not binding. It is not overly sanguine to say that the Commission has had a profound significance in Canadian—United States relations.[21]

Great Lakes Commission. In 1955 the riparian American states entered into the Great Lakes Compact to achieve greater cooperation and uniformity in the use and development of the waters and natural resources of the Great Lakes. The Commission recommends to the states measures for the orderly development of the resources of the lakes and to the federal government pertinent agreements between the United States and Canada. The Commis-

21. The Commission may also serve as an international arbitral tribunal and render a decision or finding with regard to any questions or matters of difference between the two countries involving their rights, obligations, or interests in relation to the other or the inhabitants of the other. Reference of such questions requires the conclusion of a *compromis*. This power has not been utilized. See Don C. Piper, "Two International Waterways Commissions: A Comparative Study," *Virginia Journal of International Law*, VI (1965), 109–111. For a detailed but dated study of the work of the Commission, see Chacko, *op. cit.* For a more recent, brief survey of the Commission, see L. M. Bloomfield and G. F. Fitzgerald, *Boundary Waters Problems of Canada and the United States* (Toronto: Carswell, 1958). See also Charles Clifford Dunlop, "The Origin and Development of the International Joint Commission as a Judicial Tribunal" (unpublished Master's thesis, Queen's University, 1959).

sion has concerned itself with recreational use of the lakes, pollution, fisheries problems, and water levels.

In the initial compact, there was provision for the membership of the provinces of Ontario and Quebec. The State Department objected to this provision when the compact was presented to Congress for its approval on the ground that with provincial participation the Commission entered the field of international relations; moreover the compact contained some provisions that would enable the member states to contradict the policies of the federal government. Although Congress has not yet given its approval to the compact, it has indicated that it will not approve provincial participation.[22] Since the Commission is composed of members who are not subjects of international law, it is not in a position to establish international law for the Great Lakes. However, as a voice of the riparian American states it is in a position to influence the international law concluded by the two federal governments.

Work of the International Joint Commission with Respect to the Use and Diversion of the Waters of the Great Lakes—St. Lawrence

A detailed study of the work of the International Joint Commission is not relevant here; indeed most of the work of the Commission is of a technical rather than legal nature. A brief summary of the dockets of the Commission will be a useful indication of the type of work performed by the Commission. In the period from 1912 to 1964 the Commission handled eighty-two dockets.[23] Of this number twenty-one related to the area under consideration. Of this latter number, ten dockets were joint references by both

22. See U. S., Congress, Senate, Subcommittee of Committee on Foreign Relations, *Hearings, The Great Lakes Basin,* 84th Cong., 2d Sess., 1956, pp. 6–8, 14, 17, 31–32; *idem,* Subcommittee of Committee on the Judiciary, *Hearings, Great Lakes Basin Compact,* 85th Cong., 2d Sess., 1958, p. 5.
23. See Appendix I for list of the appropriate dockets. A brief summary of dockets number 1–80 is found in Whiteman, *Digest,* III, 826–871. See also Bloomfield and Fitzgerald, *op. cit.,* pp. 58 ff.

governments for specific technical studies under the investigatory powers set forth in Article IX of the 1909 treaty. The remaining eleven dockets were for Commission approval under Article III of projects in the boundary waters. One docket was a request for approval by the United States government, one was a joint request by both governments, and nine were requests by private parties.

In its quasi-adjudicatory role, the Commission functions in a manner somewhat similar to international tribunals. It applies international law (i.e., the principles incorporated in the 1909 treaty) and it renders decisions that are binding on the parties involved, whether governmental or private. Its members are, however, generally engineers rather than jurists, and it has limited opportunity to formulate or clarify principles of international law. In its procedures for private applicants, the Commission adheres to the procedural rule of international law that private interests do not enjoy direct access to international tribunals. Accordingly private applicants must apply to the government within whose territory the desired privilege is to be exercised.[24] This does not necessarily mean that an applicant applies to his own government. It may be necessary for a national of one state to apply to the other government. In one instance a private applicant seeking to construct a bridge between Erie and Buffalo had to secure the permission of both governments.[25]

The other private applications have concerned approval for the construction or modification of works in the boundary waters utilized in hydroelectric power production.[26] In three instances Canadian and United States companies filed joint applications.

24. Such applications go either to the Department of State or to the Department of External Affairs. Each government has complete discretion to disapprove the application or to endorse it and submit it to the Commission for final approval. International Joint Commission, *Rules of Procedure and Text of Treaty* (Washington, 1947), Rule 6(b). Several individuals have attempted to file applications directly with the Commission without going through one of the governments. In such cases the Commission has refused to take any action until the appropriate government indicated its approval of the application. See Bloomfield and Fitzgerald, *op. cit.*, p. 58.

25. Docket number 21.

26. Dockets number 6, 8, 14, 15, 24, 75, 78, 79.

The joint governmental application in which the two governments sought the Commission's approval of the joint power development project in the International Rapids section of the St. Lawrence River is well known in connection with the St. Lawrence Seaway.[27] Approving the project, the Commission stipulated that the works be constructed and operated so as not to conflict with the use of the St. Lawrence River for purposes given preference over power use in the 1909 treaty (i.e., use for domestic and sanitary purposes and for navigation). The Commission also established the St. Lawrence River Joint Board of Engineers to review and co-ordinate and, if the governments authorized it, to approve the plans and specifications of the construction works. In addition the St. Lawrence River Board of Control was set up to insure that the provisions of the Commission's order relative to the water levels and the rate of discharge were followed.[28]

The special studies undertaken by the Commission at the request of both governments have related to pollution in boundary waters and in the atmosphere, the preservation of the Niagara Falls, measures necessary for power and navigation development in the St. Lawrence, and the regulation of the water level of Lake Ontario.[29] Currently the Commission is undertaking, at the request of both governments, a study of the factors that affect the water levels of the entire Great Lakes with a view to recommending appropriate measures to reduce the extreme fluctuations in the water levels.[30]

In carrying out its investigations, the Commission frequently appoints a board with representatives from both countries to conduct or organize the technical studies. In some instances national agencies undertake studies on behalf of the Commission. In all cases, the Commission's report and recommendations are not legally binding upon the governments.

27. Art. III. permits the governments to make special arrangements without obtaining the Commission's approval. The agreements providing for increased diversion at Niagara Falls are an example.

28. Docket number 68.

29. Dockets number 4, 5, 17, 54, 55, 61, 62, 67, 74.

30. Docket number 81. See Don C. Piper, "A Significant Docket for the International Joint Commission," *AJIL*, LIX (1965), 593–597.

Problems in the Use of the Boundary Waters

Since the turn of the century four problems have emerged with respect to the utilization of water resources that have involved the application of international law. The Gut Dam claims are the most recent and are being presented to a mixed claims tribunal for a final settlement. The pollution of boundary waters and the atmosphere, the preservation of the Niagara Falls and the proper diversions from the falls, and the Chicago diversion are matters that have been and remain of continuing interest to both governments.

The Gut Dam claims. Although the facts of the Gut Dam claims are unquestioned, a complex problem lies in the evaluation of the facts and the determination of legal responsibility. Part of the dam, constructed by the Canadian government in 1903 in the St. Lawrence River, extends into American territory. Consent for the construction was given by the Secretary of War following congressional authorization with the stipulation that if American property owners suffered damages as a result of the dam, the Canadian government would pay such compensation as agreed upon by it and the injured parties or as might be awarded by the appropriate United States court.[31]

The dam apparently presented no difficulties until 1952–1953 when American property owners along Lake Ontario instituted in the federal courts suits for damages against the Canadian government. They claimed that excessively high lake levels since 1947 causing damage to their property were the consequence of the Gut Dam and that the Canadian government was consequently liable for damages under the construction permit granted by the Secretary of War. The Canadian government offered to submit the problem to an arbitral tribunal, but subsequently withdrew from the negotiations when hearings on the

31. See Whiteman, *Digest*, III, 768–771.

suits commenced. In response to the suits, the Canadian Ambassador filed a suggestion of a lack of jurisdiction on the ground that the suits involved a foreign sovereign. The suits were subsequently dismissed for improper service on the ground that personal service on the Canadian government had not been accomplished by the delivery of a copy of the summons and complaint to the Consul General of Canada or someone in his office in New York.[32]

Determination of the increase in the lake level caused by the Gut Dam was one of the tasks assigned to the International Joint Commission in 1952 in its study of the water level of Lake Ontario. The Commission concluded that the dam raised the level of the lake four inches. The complex problem is how to evaluate the four-inch increase in the light of other factors that caused high water levels (e.g., rain, high wind).

In 1965 the United States and Canada, after several years of negotiations, concluded an arbitral *compromis* for the Lake Ontario Claims Tribunal—United States and Canada to handle the claims by United States nationals.[33] The task facing the tribunal is not easy. It is to determine whether Gut Dam was the cause of the damage, the nature and extent of the damage caused by the dam, the liability for payment of compensation, the amount, and who should pay it. In its determinations the Tribunal is to apply substantive law in force in Canada and the United States which includes international law. Claims will not be disallowed because of nonexhaustion of local remedies. This is the first arbitral tribunal to relate specifically to water problems arising along the Great Lakes—St. Lawrence.

Boundary water and atmospheric pollution. Within the past two decades water and atmospheric pollution in certain areas of the lakes has assumed great significance. The problem of water

32. *Oster et al.* v. *Dominion of Canada,* 144 F. Supp. 746 (1956). The court did not consider the question of sovereign immunity, but did take note of the restrictive policy of sovereign immunity set forth in the Tate letter.
33. U. S., Congress, Senate, *Gut Dam Claims Agreement with Canada,* 89th Cong., 1st Sess., 1965, Exec. C.

pollution was specifically recognized in the 1909 treaty with the
provision that boundary waters and those flowing across the
boundary would not be polluted on either side of the line to the
injury of health and property on the other side of the line. It
should be noted that the concern here is with the transboundary
movement of pollution and not with the problem as a whole and
that there is no provision for bilateral machinery to control pollution. The problem of atmospheric pollution is more recent, but
one that is also bilateral in its scope.

In attempting to control pollution in the boundary waters and
in the atmosphere, the two governments have relied upon the
International Joint Commission for studies and recommendations.
The first reference was made to the Commission in 1912 when it
investigated the causes and places of pollution of the boundary
waters which affected both countries. After several years the
Commission reported that the open lakes were essentially pure,
but that in the Detroit and Niagara rivers conditions existed that
impaired the health and welfare of citizens of both countries. In
view of this the Commission recommended that it be permitted
to promulgate rules and regulations to combat the pollution in
the boundary waters.[34] Subsequent discussions by the governments on the recommendation were not fruitful. In 1946 and
1948 both governments asked the Commission to study pollution
in the connecting rivers and channels including the Niagara River.
It found that the principle cause of pollution was the discharge of
domestic sewage and industrial wastes into the boundary waters
and tributaries.[35]

The Commission subsequently established two Advisory
Boards on Control of Pollution—one for the Superior, Huron,
Erie section, and one for the Erie-Ontario section—to maintain
continuous supervision of the boundary waters as requested by
the two governments. When pollution is observed, the Commission notifies the parties responsible. If no assurance is given that

34. Docket number 4. See Whiteman, *Digest,* III, 828–829. See Department of
State file 711.42155/334 (National Archives) for the Commission's report.
35. Dockets number 54 and 55. *Report of the International Joint Commission
on the Pollution of Boundary Waters* (1950), p. 8.

the situation will be corrected, it recommends necessary action to the appropriate government.[36]

In 1949 the Commission was asked to investigate the contribution made by vessels in the Detroit River to atmospheric pollution in the Detroit-Windsor area. The Commission recommended the adoption by the governments of certain regulations for the emission of smoke from vessels plying the river, but concluded that such fumes contributed only a minimal amount to atmospheric pollution. Industrial and transportation activities on the land areas were found to be the major source of atmospheric pollution. In this regard the Commission concluded that there was adequate legal and administrative authority in each country to enforce proper control of the emission of waste materials.[37]

Whether the International Joint Commission should be given rule-making authority with regard to pollution was the subject of extended negotiations between the two governments during the 1920's. A draft treaty prescribing substantial powers for the Commission in combating pollution was prepared by it and presented to the governments, but they were unable to agree upon a completed draft.[38] While it does not enjoy rule-making authority in maintaining its continuous supervision of boundary water pollution, the Commission is able to serve effectively in making its technical reports to the governments.

It has been mentioned that the international conventions which relate to navigation on the high seas do not relate to navigation on the Great Lakes. The same is true of the international convention for the prevention of the pollution of the sea by oil.[39] Notwith-

36. International Joint Commission, *Safeguarding Boundary Water Quality* (1961), p. 28; Whiteman, *Digest*, III, 853.
37. *Report by the International Joint Commission on the Pollution of the Atmosphere in the Detroit River Area* (1960), pp. 7–9.
38. For a text of the draft and a U. S. counter draft, see Department of State file 711.42155/411, 451 (National Archives). The U. S. objected to the initial draft because it provided that the Commission's findings as to the existence of pollution and its injurious nature would be final.
   In 1942 Canada raised the question of the resumption of the treaty negotiations that had been terminated in 1929. The State Department replied that because of the war it was not a propitious time to resume negotiations. See Department of State file 711.42155/660 (National Archives).
39. International Convention for the Prevention of Pollution of Sea by Oil, 1954, Art. II (iv). For the text of the convention, see U. S., Congress, Senate, *International Convention for the Prevention of Pollution of Sea by Oil*, 86th Cong.,

standing this fact, Canadian regulations prohibit the discharge of oil by any vessels in the Canadian waters of the Great Lakes.[40] Although the United States has statutes prohibiting the discharge of oil by merchant vessels, these are applicable only to those inland waters that are affected by the ebb and flow of the tide— thus excluding the Great Lakes.[41]

Diversion of the Niagara River and preservation of the Falls. Equitable and optimum utilization of the water flow over the Niagara Falls for hydroelectric power and the preservation of the scenic beauty of the falls cannot be accomplished unilaterally. These require the joint co-operation of the federal governments and the State of New York and the Province of Ontario. The international legal regime for the river and falls is thus a combination of special agreements between the two federal governments, the utilization of the International Joint Commission and *ad hoc* boards for technical studies, and the joint efforts of New York and Ontario in the construction of power facilities.

The Boundary Waters Treaty contained special provisions regarding the diversion of the river above the falls with the amount of water diverted from the river for power purposes limited so that the level of Lake Erie and the flow over the cataract would not be appreciably affected. This controlled diversion was to be accomplished with the least possible injury to existing power plant investments in New York and Ontario. Permissible diversion for power purposes was set at 20,000 cubic feet per second in New York and 36,000 c.f.s. in Ontario. No further diversion was to be permitted by either party; this did not apply, however, to diversions for sanitary or domestic purposes or for the service of navigation canals.[42] Within a decade after the ratification of the

---

2d Sess., 1960, Ex C. See statement by Legal Adviser Chayes before the Senate Committee on Foreign Relations, *Department of State Bulletin*, XLIV (1961), 776.

40. Canada, *Statutes at Large*, 4–5 Eliz. II, c. 34, sec. 495 (a); SOR/60–70, *The Canada Gazette*, XCIV, Part II (Feb. 24, 1960), 210.

41. 33 U.S.C. sec. 432.

42. Art. V. See Appendix E. Basically the treaty incorporates the recommendations of the International Waterways Commission. It had recommended a diversion on the Canadian side of 36,000 c.f.s. and a diversion on the American side of 18,500 c.f.s., with an additional diversion of 10,000 c.f.s. from Lake

treaty, there was pressure in the United States to increase the total diversion to 80,000 c.f.s. and to do so on a basis of equality.[43] The United States would thus obtain an additional 20,000 c.f.s. and Canada would obtain an additional 4,000 cubic feet per second. In 1923 the two governments established the Niagara River Control Board to supervise the national agencies ascertaining the amount of water diverted and to determine the accuracy of the diversion data. The Board was subsequently enlarged to constitute the Special International Niagara Board to investigate the problem of preserving the falls and to determine the amount of additional divertable water.[44] Prior to the Special Board's final report and recommendations for specific remedial works, the two governments concluded a treaty authorizing construction of remedial works and permitting an additional diversion of 10,000 c.f.s. on each side during the period from October 1 to March 31. The treaty was not perfected, however, because the United States Senate refused its consent to ratification.[45] Despite the Senate's action, the governments agreed that the remedial works should be constructed and that there should be progress toward additional and equal diversion of the river's water.[46]

In the 1940's as a result of a number of executive agreements, the permissible diversion was gradually increased on both sides

---

Michigan at Chicago. Apparently the unequal diversion was incorporated in the treaty to legalize the status quo and protect existing investments. In addition it appears to have been understood that with the majority of the water power being diverted to the Canadian side, electric power would be sold by Canadian firms to American consumers. See the "Joint Report of the International Waterways Commission on the Conditions Existing at Niagara Falls, with Recommendations" (May 3, 1906) (in document cited in n. 3, *supra*), pp. 339–340; and Department of State file 711.4216 Ni/164, 194 (National Archives).

43. See Department of State file 711.4216 Ni/134, 137, 149, 150, 190 (National Archives).

44. *For. Rel.* (1923), I, 498 ff. For the report of the Special Board, Dec. 11, 1929, see U. S., Congress, Senate, *Preservation and Improvement of the Scenic Beauty of the Niagara Falls and Rapids*, 71st Cong., 2d Sess., 1930, Doc. 128.

45. The Senate believed that the treaty and the additional diversion conferred an unwarranted advantage upon the private power company. For the text of the unperfected treaty, Jan. 2, 1929, see *For. Rel.* (1929), II, 94–97. See also *ibid.* (1936), I, 834. Prior to the signing of the treaty, the Canadian government recommended that the provision for a temporary additional diversion of 10,000 c.f.s. be incorporated in an exchange of notes rather than in a treaty. The United States indicated, however, that in view of the diversion provisions incorporated in the 1909 treaty such notes would have to be consented to by the Senate. Department of State file 711.4216 Ni/237–1/2, 296 (National Archives).

46. *For. Rel.* (1936), I, 836; *ibid.* (1938), II, 178.

of the boundary.[47] Moreover, Canada was allowed an additional diversion of 5,000 c.f.s. as compensation for an equal amount diverted into the Great Lakes from the Albany River Basin.[48] In 1950 the governments concluded a treaty providing for a maximum diversion from the Niagara River. The amount of water available for power purposes equals the total outflow from Lake Erie less that amount necessary for domestic and sanitary purposes and for the service of navigation canals. However, to preserve the scenic beauty of the falls, no diversion for power purposes is permitted which will reduce the flow over the falls to less than 100,000 c.f.s. between eight A.M. and ten P.M. during the period from April 1 to September 15, or to less than that amount from eight A.M. to eight P.M. during the period from September 16 to October 31, or to less than 50,000 c.f.s. at any other time. All excess water is available for power purposes on the basis of equality.[49] It was also agreed, apparently for the benefit of Canadian hydroelectric power interests, that until such time as there were facilities in one country to utilize its full share of the water divertable for power purposes, the other party might divert the unused portion.

The parties also agreed to ask the International Joint Commission to make recommendations as to the nature and design of the remedial works to preserve the scenic beauty of the falls; this would be in accordance with the objectives outlined in the report of the Special International Niagara Board in 1929. Following the Commission's report, in 1953 the works were constructed and subsequently completed in 1957.[50] In 1961 the two governments made

47. On May 20, 1941, an additional diversion of 5,000 c.f.s. on the American side and 3,000 c.f.s. on the Canadian side was agreed to and subsequently approved by the Senate. 55 *Stat.* 1276. In October and November of the same year additional diversions of 7,500 c.f.s. on the American side and 6,000 c.f.s. on the Canadian side were authorized for the defense effort. This was also approved by the Senate. 55 *Stat.* 1380. In 1948 Canada obtained a three-year emergency diversion of an additional 4,000 c.f.s. It was stipulated that this agreement would not be regarded as definitely in force until consented to by the Senate. *Department of State Bulletin*, XX (1949), 85.
48. See the agreement of Oct. 14, 1940, 54 *Stat.* 2426.
49. 1 U.S.T. 694. This treaty terminates paragraphs 3, 4, and 5 of Article V of the 1909 treaty and the exchange of notes of 1941 and 1948. See Appendix F.
50. Docket number 62. See Whiteman, *Digest*, III, 856–858, 771–780, 999–1002. For the Commission's report, May 5, 1953, see U. S., Congress, Subcommittee on Flood Control and Rivers and Harbors of the Senate Committee on Public Works, and the House Committee on Public Works, *Joint Hearings, Niagara Power Development*, 83rd Cong., 1st Sess., 1953, pp. 202–209.

a supplemental reference to the Commission asking for an investigation and report on measures necessary to permit compliance with the Commission's 1953 report on remedial works when full use is made of the river for power purposes. Supervision of the level of Lake Erie and the flow over the falls is maintained by the International Niagara Board of Control.

The Chicago diversion. The problem of the diversion (or more properly the withdrawal) of water from Lake Michigan at Chicago is one of the most persistent and complex problems involving the use of the waters of the Great Lakes. It raises complex international legal questions and in addition is a persistent irritant in Canadian–United States relations. Moreover, it is intertwined in matters of domestic policy with states far removed from the Great Lakes region interested in increasing the diversion. The unique factor of the Chicago diversion is not the amount of water involved, but the fact that the diverted water is not returned to the lake but enters the Mississippi River watershed. Thus the diversion represents a withdrawal or net loss of water from the Great Lakes.

To understand the international legal questions involved it is necessary to summarize briefly the basic developments in the history of the diversion, to review the provisions of the Boundary Waters Treaty, and to set forth the positions taken by the two governments on the various proposals for an increase in the diversion.[51]

The diversion began before the turn of the century. In 1889 the State of Illinois incorporated the Chicago Sanitary District to handle Chicago sewage. The District subsequently constructed a drainage canal to flush the sewage out of the city by diverting water from Lake Michigan through the Des Plains River to the Illinois River and ultimately to the Mississippi River. Although the diversion was initially for sanitary purposes, it has in more recent years been utilized primarily for the improvement of navigation in several local canals and rivers and for the production of

51. For a brief survey of the Chicago diversion with recent documents, see Whiteman, *Digest*, III, 789–812.

hydroelectric power. In 1901 when the canal was opened, the Secretary of War issued a permit for a diversion from Lake Michigan of 4,167 cubic feet per second. The effect of this diversion on the lake levels was one of the matters studied by the International Waterways Commission. In 1907 that Commission reported that a diversion of 10,000 c.f.s. at Chicago would lower the levels of the lakes and the St. Lawrence River from four and one-half to six and one-half inches. Convinced that the preservation of the lake levels was necessary for the paramount interest of navigation, the Commission recommended that the United States prohibit a diversion of more than 10,000 c.f.s. at Chicago.[52] In 1913 the Secretary of War refused to permit any diversion beyond the amount set forth in the original permit.[53] Subsequently the federal government instituted legal proceedings against the District to stop any diversion in excess of 4,167 cubic feet per second. After more than a decade of litigation, the Supreme Court, finding that the federal government could maintain the suit not only to remove obstructions to navigation but also to carry out the obligations of the 1909 treaty, declared that Illinois could not divert any water from Lake Michigan without the consent of Congress and ordered the District to stop any excess diversion.[54] Immediately following the Court's order, the District obtained a permit from the Secretary of War allowing a diversion of 8,500 cubic feet per second.[55]

During this same period Wisconsin and several other lake states sought a court injunction to prohibit Chicago from making any diversion from Lake Michigan. In 1926 the Supreme Court appointed a Master (Charles E. Hughes) to take testimony and gather evidence on the matter. He concluded that through the years the actual diversion had been at a rate of 8,500 c.f.s., resulting in the lowering of the level of Lakes Michigan and Huron by six inches and of Lakes Erie and Ontario by five

52. See the joint report of the International Waterways Commission, "The Chicago Drainage Canal" (Jan. 4, 1907) (in document cited in n. 3, *supra*), pp. 527–528.

53. For the text of the decision of the Secretary of War (Henry L. Stimson), Jan. 8, 1913, see "Papers Relating to the Chicago Drainage Canal," in Canada, *Sessional Papers*, No. 180, LX, No. 7 (1924), 113, 118, 120.

54. *Sanitary District of Chicago* v. *United States*, 266 U. S. 405, 420, 426 (1925).

55. For the Secretary's order, March 3, 1925, see *For. Rel.* (1925), I, 563.

inches.[56] In 1930 the Supreme Court ordered a gradual reduction in the diversion with a limit of 1,500 c.f.s. plus domestic pumpage effective after December 31, 1938.[57] At the present time the limit remains 1,500 cubic feet per second. With the addition of domestic pumpage, the total diversion averages 3,100 cubic feet per second.

In 1957 six of the riparian states instituted additional legal action against the State of Illinois and the Sanitary District asking the Supreme Court to reduce the diversion or limit the domestic pumpage in order to reduce the total diversion. The State of Illinois replied with a suit asking the Court to prohibit interference by the states in a new water construction project that would divert additional water from the lake. In 1959 the Court agreed to reconsider the entire question of the diversion and appointed a Special Master to gather evidence and make a report.[58] The Special Master has not yet submitted his report.

In addition to judicial action, Illinois has attempted since 1938 to obtain congressional authorization of an increased diversion. Within the past decade the District has placed special emphasis on congressional approval for an additional diversion, ostensibly for test purposes to determine the effect of an additional diversion on the other lakes. In 1954 and 1956 Congress approved an additional diversion of 1,000 c.f.s. for a three-year period, but in both instances President Eisenhower vetoed the bills.[59] Subsequent attempts have been unsuccessful in Congress.[60]

56. For the Master's report, see U. S., Congress, House, *Lake Levels, Report of the Special Master Charles E. Hughes to the Supreme Court of the United States,* 70th Cong., 1st Sess., 1928, Doc. 178, pp. 53–54.

57. *State of Wisconsin et al.* v. *State of Illinois and Sanitary District of Chicago et al.,* 278 U. S. 367 (1929); and 281 U. S. 179 (1930). Occasionally the Supreme Court has permitted additional diversions because of special conditions for short periods of time.

58. *Wisconsin et al.* v. *Illinois et al.,* Nos. 1, 2, 3, 11 Original, 360 U. S. 712, 714 (1959). The federal government has intervened in the above cases on the ground, *inter alia,* of its interest in maintaining friendly relations with Canada. The State Department has forwarded to the Special Master the note from the Canadian government of Nov. 2, 1961. See Whiteman, *Digest,* III, 803–804.

59. For the text of President Eisenhower's memorandum of disapproval, Sept. 3, 1954, see U. S., Congress, Senate, Subcommittee of Committee on Public Works, *Hearings, Diversion of Water from Lake Michigan,* 85th Cong., 2d Sess., 1958, pp. 76–77. See also *idem, Hearings, Lake Michigan Water Diversion,* 83rd Cong., 2d Sess., 1954. For the memorandum of disapproval, Aug. 9, 1956, see *Department of State Bulletin,* XXXV (1956), 357–358.

60. In order to obtain support for his legislation and ameliorate Canadian

Part of the difficulty of assessing the international legal responsibility regarding the diversion is that the 1909 treaty contains no specific provision relating to it. Although this is the case, the negotiators discussed the diversion and considered inserting into the treaty a specific provision relating to it.

In one of the preliminary drafts, the American negotiator (Chandler P. Anderson) suggested that the United States limit the amount of the Chicago diversion so that the level of the Great Lakes would not be reduced by more than eight inches. For his part, the Canadian negotiator (George Gibbons) suggested a diversion of no more than 10,000 cubic feet per second. The final text omitted any reference to the diversion at the insistence of the then Secretary of State (Elihu Root).[61]

In a memorandum for the Senate Foreign Relations Committee, Anderson indicated that it was his intention in drafting the treaty that the provision for legal remedies incorporated in Article II would be inapplicable to the Chicago diversion since it was an existing case. Moreover, he pointed out:

> The treaty therefore recognizes that the settlement of the question of the use of the waters of Lake Michigan is purely a domestic question and leaves undisturbed the governmental rights of the United States with respect to it. But this is the view of Great Britain and Canada as shown by the last paragraph of the article [II] which reserves to each of the high contracting parties any right which it may now have to object to any interference with or diversion of waters on the other side

objections, Senator Douglas of Illinois visited Ottawa in 1959 and talked to Canadian Prime Minister Diefenbaker about the diversion. Subsequently he declared that the District and the State of Illinois were willing to compensate Canada for any loss to its shipping and power interests that could be ascribed to the additional diversion. Canada would have to prove its losses before an *ad hoc* international tribunal on which both countries would have equal representation. Although Senator Douglas may have taken his proposal seriously, the Committee did not and no mention of it was made in its report to the Senate. See U. S., Congress, House, Committee on Public Works, *Hearings, Lake Michigan Water Diversion*, 86th Cong., 1st Sess., 1959; *idem, Requiring a Study to be Conducted of the Effect of Increasing the Diversion of Water from Lake Michigan into the Illinois Waterway for Navigation and for Other Purposes*, 86th Cong., 1st Sess., 1959, Rept. 191; U. S., Congress, Senate, Subcommittee of Committee on Public Works, *Hearings, Water Diversion from Lake Michigan*, 86th Cong., 1st Sess., 1959, pp. 7–8, 24; *idem, Diversion of Water from Lake Michigan at Chicago*, 86th Cong., 1st Sess., 1959, Report 808; and Canada, House of Commons, *Parliamentary Debates*, 1959, pp. 2966–2967.

61. See Document 118 (cited in n. 7, *supra*), pp. 37, 41. See especially p. 37 for the text of Anderson's preliminary draft, and Appendix E for the text of the treaty.

of the boundary, the effect of which would be productive of material injury to the navigation interests on its own side of the boundary. This provision relates to public interests in distinction to private interests, and would be wholly unnecessary if under the preceding provisions of the article any right was given to recover damages for injuries to public interests on the other side of the line.[62]

In an appearance before the same committee, Secretary of State Root declared that the terms of the treaty were very carefully written so as to exclude Lake Michigan and the Chicago diversion. He implied that the reason why all references to the diversion were omitted was that Canada obtained a diversion of 36,000 c.f.s. from the Niagara River and the United States only 20,000 c.f.s.[63]

It appears from the correspondence relating to the treaty negotiations that the negotiators agreed that the diversion was governed by Article II of the treaty. Accordingly it was a matter wholly within the jurisdiction of the United States, except that the Canadian government possessed the right to object to any diversion that produced "material injury" to the navigation interests on its side of the boundary. It has been mentioned that although the Canadian Prime Minister was unhappy about the article and the diversion, Gibbons, the negotiator, was convinced that international law accorded the United States the right to make the diversion.

On occasion, it has been tentatively suggested by authorities of both parties that Article III of the treaty is applicable to the Chicago diversion.[64] If so, the approval of the International Joint

62. For the text of his memorandum, see Department of State file 711.42155/151 (National Archives); or U. S., Congress, House, Committee on Rivers and Harbors, *Hearings, Illinois and Mississippi Rivers, and Diversion of Water from Lake Michigan,* 68th Cong., 1st Sess., 1924, pp. 1294–1298. Perhaps an argument could be made that the diversion of 4,167 c.f.s. was the existing diversion at the time of the ratification of the treaty. Thus any diversion greater than that amount might be characterized as a new, rather than an existing diversion. If this were the case, the provision with regard to legal remedies might apply to injuries suffered as a result of a diversion greater than 4,167 c.f.s.

63. U. S., Congress, Senate, Committee on Foreign Relations, *Hearings and Proceedings on Treaty between United States and Canada Concerning Boundary Waters,* 61st Cong., 2d Sess. (1910), pp. 3–5.

64. See the Canadian note, April 9, 1959, in Senate Hearings, 1959 (cited in n. 60, *supra*), pp. 162–163; the Department's letter, July 26, 1956, in Senate Hearings, 1958 (cited in n. 59, *supra*), p. 357; and the Solicitor's memorandum, June 3, 1926, in Department of State file 711.4216 M58/103–1/2 (National Archives). In

Commission would be required for any non-existent use or diversion of the waters of Lake Michigan. Such suggestions have not been developed and would appear to be questionable. Article III applies specifically to boundary waters—those waters through which the international boundary line passes; this point was emphasized by Anderson in his memorandum prepared for the Senate Foreign Relations Committee.[65] The order of precedence listed in Article VIII of the treaty is also inapplicable to Lake Michigan since it applies only to boundary waters.

A study of the treaty and analysis of the correspondence relating to the negotiations supports the conclusion that Article II of the treaty accords to the United States the legal right to make a diversion at Chicago, but it does not accord a right to divert an unlimited quantity of water. Canada may object to the diversion if it produces "material injury" to navigation interests on its side of the line. Two difficult problems thus emerge that engender controversy. At what point does the diversion produce "material injury" to Canadian navigation interests? The treaty provides no criteria for making this judgment. Second, what legal weight must the United States accord to Canadian protests? The treaty does not provide any guidance.

With this background of the treaty and the diversion, we can appraise the various positions taken by both governments in their exchanges of notes. It is important to note that the public record does not indicate any disagreement or protest relative to the present diversion of 3,100 cubic feet per second.[66] Statements of governmental policy and exchanges of notes are generally the consequence of proposals to increase the existing diversion. Reports prepared by hydraulic engineers indicate that a permanent increase of 1,000 c.f.s. in the diversion would lower Lakes Michi-

---

Sanitary District of Chicago v. *United States,* Mr. Justice Holmes erroneously implied that a diversion from Lake Michigan required the consent of the International Joint Commission and the Dominion of Canada. 266 U. S. 405 (1925).

65. See his memorandum in Department of State file 711.42155/151 (National Archives).

66. The present diversion of 1,500 c.f.s. plus domestic pumpage was approved in the unperfected Great Lakes—St. Lawrence Deep Waterway Treaty. In addition that treaty provided that no future diversion into another watershed would be made without the authorization of the IJC. See *For. Rel.* (1932), II, 74–75 and Appendix H.

gan and Huron by .08 feet in fifteen years and Lakes Erie and Ontario by .05 feet. The power loss at Niagara and in the St. Lawrence would be about .04 per cent of the total energy production. The carrying capacity of the United States Great Lakes fleet would be reduced by approximately 300,000 tons.[67]

Since 1912, when the Secretary of War was asked to permit a diversion greater than 4,167 c.f.s., the Canadian government has consistently opposed any proposed additional diversion of water from Lake Michigan. Its objections have varied but in general they are based on the potential injury to Canadian navigation and hydroelectric power interests. The emphasis placed on the principles of international law, general treaty commitments, and neighborly goodwill has varied.

In 1913 it was alleged that a proposed increased diversion would adversely affect navigation on the Great Lakes and thus infringe Canadian rights of navigation in the channels of the St. Lawrence River and the Detroit River guaranteed by Article VII of the Webster–Ashburton Treaty. In addition navigation rights in the boundary waters and Lake Michigan, secured under Article I of the 1909 treaty, would also be adversely affected.[68] This view was shared by the Secretary of War, who refused the request for an additional diversion on the ground that it would cause substantial injury to navigation interests. In his decision, the Secretary pointed out that the problem was not merely national but international. Furthermore, a reading of Article X of the 1909 treaty (providing for the reference of questions and matters of difference between the United States and Canada to the International Joint Commission for a decision) convinced him that an administrative officer should not authorize, in the face of Canadian protests, a diversion which would be injurious to Canadian interests.[69]

In 1926 Canada reminded the United States that "neighborly

67. U. S., Army, Corps of Engineers, *Effect on Great Lakes and St. Lawrence River of an Increase of 1,000 Cubic Feet per Second in the Diversion at Chicago* (1957), pp. 58–63. In monetary terms the loss of power would be $750,000 annually and the loss to U. S. shipping $240,000 annually.

68. See the Canadian brief to the Secretary of War in Borden Papers, M.G. 26 H, RLB No. 560, item 102115 (Public Archives of Canada).

69. See n. 53, *supra*.

goodwill" and the 1909 treaty led to the conclusion that no diversion from one watershed to another could be made without joint consideration and agreement.[70] Occasional mention has been made of the general principles of international law and the incompatibility of any increased diversion with those principles. In 1913 Canada announced: ". . . the authorities of the United States or the authorities of any State have not under the recognized principles of International Law any right to divert from Lake Michigan by any means, or for any purpose, such an amount of water as will prejudicially affect the navigation of boundary waters in which both Canada and the United States are deeply and vitally interested."[71] It should be noted that the Canadian note was cautious in its statement of the rules of international law. It did not say that the principles of international law prohibited any American diversion; rather, it said that the principles did not give it any right to do so. Subsequently the Canadian government claimed that it was a "recognized principle of international practice" (not law) that a diversion from one watershed naturally tributary to the waters forming a part of the international boundary to another could not be made without the consent of the co-riparian state.[72]

Notwithstanding the occasional references to the general principles of international law and practice, the Canadian notes emphasize that an increased diversion would result in the injury of Canadian navigation and power interests and the violation of several treaties and agreements between the two governments.[73] With regard to the latter, the Canadian government in its recent notes asserts that the following treaties or agreements would be violated: the 1909 Boundary Waters Treaty (either Article II or III, whichever is considered to be applicable); the Niagara River Treaty, which was predicated on the assumption that the existing

70. See the note of May 1, 1926, in *For. Rel.* (1926), I, 585.

71. See the note of March 17, 1913 (in document cited in n. 53, *supra*), p. 126; see also the note of April 22, 1921, in *ibid.*, p. 128.

72. See *ibid.*; and note of Feb. 5, 1926, in *For. Rel.* (1926), I, 582.

73. See, for example, the note of March 21, 1924, wherein it is stated that the diversion would "adversely affect navigation on the Great Lakes and the St. Lawrence River as well as the actual or prospective development of power upon river and inter-lake connecting waters." *For. Rel.* (1924), I, 352.

water supply would be preserved; the exchanges of notes relative to the construction of the St. Lawrence Seaway, which are based on the understanding that there would not be unilateral action repugnant to the purposes of the seaway; the exchange of notes relative to the Canadian diversion from the Albany River Basin into the Great Lakes; and the orders of the International Joint Commission relative to power development in Quebec and Ontario, which assume a diversion of 3,100 c.f.s. at Chicago.[74]

In their strong opposition to the bills authorizing an increased diversion for test purposes, Canadian authorities have pointed out that the effect of the diversion can be determined theoretically; consequently there is no need for a temporary diversion for test purposes. In their view, the purpose of the test diversion is to facilitate additional permanent diversions. Consequently they have expressed unalterable opposition to any bill to increase the amount of water diverted either temporarily or permanently.

The assertion by the Canadian government that a unilateral increase in the diversion would impair existing facilities and violate several treaties and agreements has substantial merit and appears to have been accepted by the United States.

In replying to the Canadian representations, the Department of State is caught in the middle and confronted with two tasks. Not only must it present the position of the United States *vis a vis* Canada but it is also called upon to present its views and those of the Canadian government to Congress relative to the bills for an increased diversion.

With regard to its former task, the Department has apparently not presented an extended reply to the Canadian legal arguments but has instead merely indicated its disagreement with the Canadian interpretation of the legal issues and its disposition not to enter into any extended legal discussion of the Chicago diver-

74. See the note of March 10, 1954, in Senate Hearings, 1954 (cited in n. 59, *supra*), p. 26; note of Feb. 13, 1956, in U. S., Congress, Senate, Subcommittee of Committee on Public Works, *Hearings, Lake Michigan Water Diversions,* 84th Cong., 2d Sess., 1956, p. 64; and the aide memoire, Feb. 20, 1959, in Whiteman, *Digest,* III, 795; the note of April 9, 1959, in *ibid.,* pp. 796–797; and the note of Nov. 2, 1961, in *ibid.,* pp. 803–804. For a summary by the Department of State of the Canadian position, see the letter of the Assistant Secretary of State (Macomber) to the Chairman of the Senate Committee on Foreign Relations (Fulbright), Feb. 15, 1960, in *ibid.,* pp. 798–801.

sion.[75] In recent appearances before Senate and House committees, the Department representatives have indicated that, although they do not agree with the Canadian arguments, they are
not in a position to question Canada's representations.[76] It is
evident from Departmental memoranda that during the 1920's
(when the amount of water diverted was approximately 8,500
c.f.s.) the Department Solicitor believed that Canada had certain
rights with regard to the amount of water diverted from Lake
Michigan which the United States had to consider. Furthermore,
he concluded that in the opinion of most authorities on international law the United States, in the light of the existing Canadian
interests, was under an obligation to prevent any act which would
impair full and free navigation on the Great Lakes. In this regard
he declared: "It seems obvious that Canada is possessed of rights
in the boundary waters, and in Lake Michigan, which are assured
by law and by the terms of the Treaty of 1909, and that the
diversions from Lake Michigan at Chicago sufficiently affect such
rights as to require this Government, upon objection, to effect a
remedy."[77] The Solicitor also rejected the Harmon doctrine and
concluded: "Canada has substantial rights in respect of the waters of Lake Michigan which must be respected, and . . . these
rights are recognized at least by implication in the second paragraph of Article 2 of the Boundary Waters Treaty of 1909. . . ."[78]
Apparently these views were never officially made known to the
Canadian government.

Since the 1930's the Department has consistently opposed the
bills authorizing an increased diversion at Chicago. The reasons
for its opposition have varied, ranging from policy considerations

75. See the notes of Oct. 17, 1927, in *For. Rel.* (1927), I, 486; and June 12,
1959, in Whiteman, *Digest,* III, 798. In 1924 in response to an enquiry from the
Department of Justice whether Canadian authorities might desire to appear before
the Supreme Court in the *Sanitary* case, the Department of State replied that it
had not accepted the Canadian legal arguments and did not feel that they should
be presented before the Supreme Court since the United States might want to
contest them at a later date. See Department of State file 711.4216 M58/47
(National Archives).

76. See Senate Report 808 (cited in note 60, *supra*), p. 17; and Senate Hearings, 1959 (cited in n. 60, *supra*), pp. 164–165.

77. See the Solicitor's memorandum, June 3, 1926, in Department of State file
711.4216 M58/103–1/2 (National Archives).

78. See the Solicitor's note, June 5, 1926, in Department of State file 711.4216
M58/97 (National Archives).

to legal principles. One reason regularly advanced by the executive branch is that the United States should refrain from taking
unilateral action on such a matter in the face of Canadian protests. This was one reason given by President Eisenhower in
vetoing a bill in 1954 calling for a test diversion of 2,500 cubic
feet per second.[79] Two decades earlier President Roosevelt expressed the same view.[80] In recent years the Department has
urged that the principle of joint action prevail in matters between
the two countries; for this reason it has opposed increased diversion on the basis of policy considerations and not necessarily on
the basis of a legal interpretation of the matter.[81]

Despite its desire to eschew legal arguments, the Department
has indicated that it believes that there is a strong body of legal
precedent supporting the view that the United States may not
authorize an additional diversion from Lake Michigan without
reference to Canadian interests.[82] Specifically it indicated that the
increased diversion might conflict with American obligations in
Articles II, III, and VIII of the 1909 treaty and Article VI of the
1950 treaty. Even if these treaty provisions were believed to be
inapplicable to Lake Michigan, the general principles of international law, as recognized by the United States, regarding the use
of boundary waters would be violated by unilateral diversion, if
carried out in the light of Canadian objections.[83] Notwithstanding

79. For the text of his veto message, Sept. 3, 1954, see Senate Hearings, 1958
(cited in n. 59, *supra*), pp. 76–77.
80. *For. Rel.* (1934), I, 967. See also Department of State file 711.4216
M58/198, 200 (National Archives).
81. See Senate Hearings, 1956 (cited in n. 74, *supra*), p. 54. In this same matter,
the Canadian-American Interparliamentary Group meeting in 1959 agreed that unilateral action should not be taken in any matter affecting the interests of both
countries without discussions to reconcile the different views. See U. S., Congress,
House, *Report of the Second Meeting of the Canada-United States Interparliamentary Group*, 86th Cong., 1st Sess., 1959, Report 730, p. 7.
82. See Senate Hearings, 1956 (cited in n. 74, *supra*), p. 62. This view is
supported by a former member of the Office of the Legal Adviser, William Roy
Vallance, who worked closely with U. S.—Canadian problems. He declares that
there is a considerable body of legal precedent in support of the position that the
United States cannot authorize additional diversions without approval by the
Canadian government. See "The Settlement of International Boundary Waters
Questions in North America," *Cursos Monográficos*, VII (1959), 289.
83. See the Department's letter, July 26, 1956, in Senate Hearings, 1958 (cited
in n. 59, *supra*), p. 357; also the statement of the Assistant Legal Adviser
(Kearney) that "the trend in international law is strongly toward the establish-
ment of the principle that an upstream riparian state cannot deal with the waters

this position, an Acting Legal Adviser (Raymond) did indicate that the 1909 treaty did not affect the legal rights of Canadian interests with regard to the Chicago diversion. Those Canadian interests injured by the diversion could not rely on the terms of the 1909 treaty for relief but only on the general principles of international law.[84]

Just as the 1909 treaty does not provide specific guidelines for the Chicago diversion, the general rules of customary international law relating to the non-navigable use of international rivers fail to provide such guide lines.[85] In addition to the *Lake Lanoux* case there are a number of resolutions or suggestions by publicists or study groups with regard to the substance of the law, but, as Mr. Justice Cardozo suggested in another context, they need the *imprimatur* of a court to attest their jural quality.[86]

Although the resolutions and suggestions mentioned above differ in some respects, they contain some common ideas. First, a riparian making a diversion of waters within its jurisdiction that are a part of a common waterway must recognize and consider the interests and rights of the co-riparians. Second, a riparian state

---

within its borders which cross its boundary to a downstream riparian state in such a way as to seriously impair the rights or interests of the downstream riparian state." U. S., Congress, Senate, Committee on Foreign Relations, *Hearings, Columbia River Treaty,* 87th Cong., 1st Sess. (1961), Exec. C, p. 39.

84. See Senate Hearings, 1958 (cited in n. 59, *supra*), pp. 108–109. Another reason candidly admitted by the Department to have influenced its position on the diversion problem was the matter of the diversion of the Columbia River. In this instance, the respective positions of the two parties were completely reversed, with the Canadian government claiming a right to make an unlimited diversion from the Kootenay River within Canadian jurisdiction. Unilateral action by the United States with regard to Lake Michigan was seen as an unfortunate precedent for the Columbia River diversion. *Ibid.,* p. 357.

85. The United States does not regard the Harmon doctrine as a proper statement of the general principles of law. See the statement of the Assistant to the Legal Adviser (English) during the hearings on the treaty with Mexico, in U. S., Congress, Senate, Committee on Foreign Relations, *Hearings, Water Treaty with Mexico,* 79th Cong., 1st Sess., 1945, part 5, p. 1751.

86. See the following for statements regarding the non-navigable use of international rivers: *Lake Lanoux* case (France v. Spain), *AJIL,* LIII (1959), 156–171; document 118 (cited in n. 7, *supra*), pp. 89–91; F. J. Berber, *Rivers in International Law* (New York: Oceana, 1959), pp. 11–44; L'Institut de Droit International, *Annuaire,* XXIV (1911), 365; Clyde Eagleton, "The Use of Waters of International Rivers," *The Canadian Bar Review,* XXXIII (1955), 1021, 1025; Herbert Arthur Smith, *The Economic Uses of International Rivers* (London: P. S. King and Son, 1931), p. 51; International Law Association, *Report of the Forty-Seventh Conference, Dubrovnik, 1956,* pp. 241–243, and International Law Association, *Report on the Forty-Eighth Conference, New York, 1958,* p. 100.

may act unilaterally in such a matter so long as its action does not cause substantial injury to the interests of the co-riparian states. Third, a riparian state is under a duty to consult and obtain an agreement with the co-riparian states, if they are willing to do so; however, the co-riparian states do not have a veto over the former's actions. If the co-riparian states are unwilling to obtain a proper solution by consultation or other means as enumerated in the United Nations Charter, the riparian state is no longer obliged to refrain from unilateral action.

These tentative principles do not appear to contradict in any way the provisions of the 1909 treaty. On the contrary, the evidence appears to support the conclusion that the positions assumed by both governments, the principles incorporated in the treaty, and the general principles of customary international law are compatible.

Despite the fact that both governments are parties to the optional clause of the Statute of the International Court of Justice, there is no evidence that either government has ever considered taking a contentious case to the Court for an interpretation of the treaty or a statement of the pertinent rules of customary international law. This is not surprising; the history of Canadian–United States relations shows a predisposition to handle problems through diplomatic channels or to create commissions or *ad hoc* tribunals.

Both governments have also shown great reluctance to refer the diversion problem to the International Joint Commission for an investigation and report. Occasional offers to utilize the Commission or other bodies have not materialized.[87] In making its study of the water level of Lake Ontario, the Commission was authorized to study the various factors influencing the water level including diversions into or out of the lakes. The Commission thus took note of the Chicago diversion in relation to the diversion into

---

87. In 1913 the Canadian government indicated that it reserved the right to raise the question whether the diversion should be referred to the Commission. See document cited in n. 68, *supra*. In 1924 the United States also indicated its willingness to refer the diversion problem to a joint board of engineers with the understanding that any such reference would be without prejudice to its rights with reference to the diversion or to its position concerning questions which might arise because of the diversion. *For. Rel.* (1924), I, 355.

the lakes through the Long Lac-Ogoki works but did not make any recommendations. The recent reference to the Commission to undertake a study of the water levels of the lakes as a whole places the Chicago diversion before the Commission as part of the larger problem of stabilizing the water levels on all the lakes. Whether the Commission will recommend that specific limitations be placed on the diversion remains to be seen.[88]

Diversions into the Great Lakes—St. Lawrence. The Chicago diversion of water out of the Great Lakes—St. Lawrence is one-half of the diversion problem. Since 1940 Canada has been diverting approximately 5,000 c.f.s. into Lake Superior from the Albany River Basin. This diversion is set forth in exchanges of notes with the provision that Canada is entitled to an equal amount of water at Niagara for power purposes. Thus the principle that water diverted into the system is vested in the government from whose territory it comes is clearly established.[89] If it is technically possible and economically feasible to divert additional Canadian waters into the system to the benefit of United States interests, it seems clear that some type of compensation by the United States would be required.

88. See Piper, *AJIL*, LIX, 593–597.
89. 54 *Stat.* 2426. This same principle was set forth in the unperfected Great Lakes—St. Lawrence Deep Waterway Treaty. See Appendix H.

7

Limitation of Naval Armaments

One well-known aspect of the legal regime for the lakes is the Rush-Bagot Agreement that provides for the limitation of naval armaments on the lakes. Although this exchange of notes is now primarily of historical interest, it is worthy of consideration in light of the fact that it is part of the conventional law between the two states. Moreover it illustrates problems that may be encountered in the formulation and interpretation of arms limitation agreements.

In their exchange of notes, the governments agreed that they would limit their naval forces on Lake Ontario to one vessel of one hundred tons with one eighteen-pound cannon; on the upper lakes (which apparently encompassed Lake Michigan) the limit was two vessels of like size and armament; for Lake Champlain, the limit was one vessel of like size and armament. In addition the agreement provided for the dismantling of all other naval vessels on the lakes with the stipulation that neither party would construct or arm any other naval vessels on the lakes' shores.[1]

The agreement applied only to naval forces on the lakes and not to military forces on the shores of the lakes nor to the remaining portion of the international boundary. Understandably, the agreement did have the effect of diminishing the value and utility of fortifications on the lakes' shores. It was also inapplicable to the islands located in the lakes. In 1850 when the United States

1. Rush-Bagot Agreement, April 28, 1817. 8 *Stat.* 231. See also Department of State file 711.42155/501 (National Archives) for the Department's position regarding the applicability of the agreement to Lake Michigan.

obtained Horseshoe Reef from the British, it did so on the specific understanding that it would not fortify the reef.[2]

Although the agreement was not concluded until 1817, there were several earlier but unsuccessful attempts to arrive at such an understanding. During the peace negotiations (1782), John Adams suggested a prohibition of naval forces on the lakes and military fortifications along the frontier. Since nothing of substance resulted from his suggestion, John Jay, during the 1794 negotiations, proposed that both countries remove all military troops from within a limited distance from the lakes. Unfortunately nothing resulted from this proposal.[3]

During the negotiations leading to the Treaty of Ghent, the British Commissioners astounded their American colleagues by demanding that the United States unilaterally refrain from maintaining any naval vessels on the lakes and any fortifications along the lakes' shores. Such a stipulation, they declared, was necessary to preserve Canadian security and integrity. The proposal was, of course, wholly unacceptable to the American Commissioners. Fortunately, the British did not make the stipulation a *sine qua non* and the treaty was concluded without any reference to disarmament on the lakes.[4]

Following the ratification of the Treaty of Ghent, the United States proposed a reciprocal arrangement for the limitation of naval forces on the lakes. The arrangement was accepted and was incorporated into an exchange of notes with both parties initiating immediate action to give effect to its stipulations. One year later, in April, 1818, President Monroe submitted the agreement to the Senate for consideration of the question "whether this is

2. 18 *Stat.* (2) 325. During the boundary dispute concerning Fox, Stony, and Sugar Islands, the United States declared that it would accept a provision not to fortify the islands only if there were a reciprocal treaty applicable to all islands in the mouth of the Detroit River. William R. Manning, *Diplomatic Correspondence of the United States: Canadian Relations, 1784–1860* (Washington: Carnegie Endowment for International Peace, 1942), II, 7–8, 318.

3. Edgar W. McInnis, *The Unguarded Frontier* (New York: Doubleday, Doran, 1942), p. 145; and Henry P. Johnston, ed., *The Correspondence and Public Papers of John Jay* (New York: Putnam, 1893), IV, 17.

4. James Morton Callahan, *American Foreign Policy in Canadian Relations* (New York: Macmillan, 1937), p. 76; Manning, *op. cit.*, I, 630–631, 639, 643, 653, 662.

such an arrangement as the Executive is competent to enter into, by the powers vested in it by the Constitution, or is it such an one as required the advice and consent of the Senate." Avoiding the delicate question, the Senate gave its consent and approval and recommended that the agreement be carried into effect by the President.[5]

In the early years of the agreement both parties engaged in unilateral actions which threatened to destroy it. In 1838 when the activities of the "Canadian Patriots" prompted British augmentation of naval forces on the lakes, the United States did not protest since the augmentation was characterized as self-defense.[6] Within a few years, however, it did protest the purported British construction of naval vessels on the lakes' shores and called for a strict compliance with the terms of the agreement. Because of the purported British buildup, Congress authorized the construction of the 498-ton *Michigan* to be maintained on the lakes. Its presence in turn elicited several British protests and reminders of the necessity of reciprocal adherence to the agreement.[7]

During the Civil War the United States increased its naval force on the lakes because of the depredations of Confederate raiders based in Canada. In justifying its action, it explained that the agreement was intended to prevent either party from maintaining a naval force which would endanger the security of the other, but it did not contemplate the possible intervention of a third party ill-disposed to both.[8]

Because of continued depredations by Confederate raiders and Canadian impotence in preventing the raids, the United States, in November, 1864, gave notice of its intention to terminate the agreement at the expiration of a six-month period. The military situation improved, however, and the notice of termination was withdrawn prior to the expiration of the six-month period. This latter notice was given notwithstanding the fact that Congress

5. *Ibid.*, 235, 783, 786, 790, 792, 794, 802; David Hunter Miller, ed., *Treaties and Other International Acts of the United States of America* (Washington: Government Printing Office, 1931), II, 645–649; *American State Papers, Foreign Relations*, IV, 202 ff.
6. Manning, *op. cit.*, III, 151–158, 474–475.
7. *Ibid.*, pp. 157–158, 888–889. See also 5 *Stat.* 460.
8. *For. Rel.* (1864), II, 715–717; *ibid.* (1865), I, 5, 7.

had passed a joint resolution approving the notice of termination. The constitutional question raised by the conflicting action was regarded by a subsequent Secretary of State (Foster) as opening the door to a "nice argument" but one which was "more interesting than material." Whatever the domestic complications, both parties believed that the agreement remained in force.[9]

Throughout the history of the agreement, the United States has occasionally made unilateral interpretations that have irritated Canadian authorities. In this regard, Prime Minister Mackenzie King is reported to have said: ". . . the truth is our American friends have been steadily evading [it], until it has become more or less of a mockery to speak of its terms in the manner in which we do." [10]

Although the agreement is silent on the matter, the United States has always insisted that revenue cutters are beyond the scope of the commitment. In 1892 the then Secretary of State (Foster) declared that it had been tacitly understood by both parties that such cutters were beyond the purview of the agreement. Such an understanding, he declared, was consonant with the spirit of the instrument. (At that time the United States maintained three cutters on the lakes, each of which exceeded the specific tonnage and armament limits.)[11] During the exchanges in 1922 relative to a new treaty, both parties agreed that revenue and police cutters should be exempt from the provisions of any disarmament treaty.[12]

Another matter on which the United States acted unilaterally was that of employing naval training vessels on the lakes. Since the agreement is silent on this point, the United States took the position that the use of naval vessels for training purposes was not

9. *For. Rel.* (1864), II, 338, 668; *ibid.* (1865), I, 197; *ibid.*, II, 175, 192. For the Congressional resolution see, J. R. 13 in Appendix to *Congressional Globe*, 38th Cong., 2d Sess., 1865, p. 159. See also U. S., Congress, House, *War Vessels on the Great Lakes*, 56th Cong., 1st Sess., 1900, Doc. 471, pp. 36–37.

10. Quoted by James Eayrs, "'A Low Dishonest Decade': Aspects of Canadian External Policy, 1931–1939," in Hugh L. Keenleyside *et al., The Growth of Canadian Policies in External Affairs* (Durham, N. C.: Duke University Press, 1960), p. 64.

11. Document 471 (cited in note 9, *supra*), pp. 34–35. As early as 1815, Congress authorized the President to dismantle all naval vessels on the Great Lakes except revenue cutters. 3 *Stat.* 217.

12. *For. Rel.* (1923), I, 488.

contrary to the spirit of the understanding. The question first arose in 1861 when the British inquired about the presence of the *Michigan* on the lakes. Declaring that the vessel was used solely for training purposes, the United States indicated that it believed that such usage was permissible. At the turn of the century the American government reiterated its belief that the employment of training vessels on the lakes was "not necessarily hostile to the spirit of the arrangement."[13]

Two decades later, after the conclusion of the Washington Naval Arms Limitation Conference, Prime Minister Mackenzie King expressed objections to the sixteen armed American vessels employed on the lakes for training purposes. Because Canada could not equal such a training force, the Prime Minister wanted the situation changed and proposed in his draft of a new treaty that training vessels be excluded from the lakes, including Lake Michigan. In its counter-draft, the United States advocated the employment of training vessels on the lakes on the condition that they would never be used for hostile purposes on the lakes—even in wartime.[14]

With the approach of World War II this matter became of vital importance. In an exchange of notes in 1939 it was agreed that it was "clearly within the letter as well as the spirit of the agreement for naval vessels of both parties to be employed in the training of naval reserves or in any other normal activity. . . ."[15] After the war a similar understanding was agreed to by the governments on the recommendation of the Permanent Joint Board on Defense.[16]

Unilateral action by the United States was taken on one other matter—that of construction of naval vessels on the lakes. On this subject the agreement specifically provides that "no other vessels of war shall be there built or armed." Strict compliance with this requirement was observed until the turn of the century. After the

13. Document 471 (cited in note 9, *supra*), pp. 3, 27–28. See Department of State file 711.42131/33, 39, 42, 46 (National Archives); and Governor General file R.G. 7, G. 21, No. 192E (Public Archives of Canada) for notes concerning transit of naval training vessels through Canadian waters to the Great Lakes.
14. *For. Rel.* (1923), I, 484–494.
15. 61 *Stat.* 4069.
16. 61 *Stat.* 4082; see also Whiteman, *Digest*, III, 741–752.

breakdown of negotiations with the British in 1899, the United States, impressed with the advantages to be gained by permitting naval construction on the lakes, announced that it regarded such construction as compatible with the agreement so long as the vessels were not utilized to increase the permanent armament on the lakes.[17]

In their exchange of drafts in 1922 both countries agreed that construction of naval vessels should be permitted provided the other party was informed of the construction and no armament was installed on a vessel so long as it remained on the lakes.[18] This understanding was formally stated in an exchange of notes in 1939.[19] After Canada entered World War II, it was agreed that gun mounts and armament could be installed on vessels being constructed on the lakes, provided the armament was in such condition that it could not be used while the vessels were on the lakes.[20] It was further agreed, after the United States became a belligerent, that naval vessels could be constructed, fully armed, and combat tested while on the lakes.[21]

Because of the developments in shipbuilding and naval armaments, several suggestions have been made over the past century as to the desirability of revising the 1817 instrument. Apparently, however, neither party has suggested taking any action under the plea of *rebus sic stantibus*. The first suggestion for a revision came in 1844 and was motivated by the development of the steamship; however, nothing came of the suggestion.[22] In the 1890's the

---

17. See Governor General file R.G. 7, G. 21, No. 192A, Vol. I(a) (Public Archives of Canada). In 1890 the Secretary of Navy indicated that a contract for a naval vessel could not be awarded to the low bidder because the 1817 agreement prohibited construction of naval vessels on the lakes. See *Report of the Secretary of the Navy, 1890*, p. 8. See also Document 471 (cited in note 9, *supra*), pp. 3, 67–68, 71–72. See Department of State file 711.4213/23 (National Archives), for a Navy query, April 8, 1911, whether sea-going tugs (unarmed) could be built on the Great Lakes. The Department answered in the affirmative on the understanding that upon completion they would be removed and were not intended to be armed.
18. *For. Rel.* (1923), I, 484 ff.
19. 61 *Stat.* 4069.
20. 61 *Stat.* 4077.
21. 61 *Stat.* 4080.
22. The initial suggestion came from the Secretary of Navy; see Manning, *op. cit.*, III, 263–265.

United States favored a revision which would permit construction of naval vessels on the lakes, but this met with strong opposition in Canada.[23]

The most serious attempt at revision came in 1922 after the conclusion of the Washington Conference on the Limitation of Armaments, when the Canadian Prime Minister Mackenzie King indicated a desire to draft a new treaty. Although apparently surprised by the suggestion, Secretary of State Hughes indicated a willingness to enter into negotiations. A Canadian draft was submitted immediately with a request that signature of the treaty be accomplished by January 31, 1924, so that the treaty might be submitted to Parliament on its opening day. Negotiations for the new treaty ended with the presentation of the American counterdraft that differed in some respects from the Canadian draft, especially on the matter of training vessels on the lakes.[24]

Although revision of the agreement may have been desirable in 1922, it was agreed in 1939 that any revision was undesirable. Notwithstanding the fact that its specific technical provisions had long since become obsolete, the agreement had assumed over the years a "symbolic importance" which precluded any formal revision.[25] As a result exchanges of notes were initiated to modify its terms to meet wartime demands.

Although the Rush-Bagot Agreement is nearly a century and a half old, it is, of course, a modest achievement in the total context of arms limitation. Despite the simplicity of its provisions, the agreement became technically obsolete within a few decades after its conclusion, with the consequence that its specific technical provisions were violated, especially by the United States. In most instances the violation of the agreement was not malicious

23. Document 471 (cited in note 9, *supra*), p. 38. In 1898 a Joint High Commission was established to consider points at issue between the United States and Canada, including the 1817 agreement, but the negotiations broke down over the Alaskan boundary and the agreement was never considered. See Governor General file (cited in note 17, *supra*); and Canada, *Naval Vessels on the Great Lakes Correspondence* (1892–1917) (Ottawa, n.d.).

24. See *For. Rel.* (1923), I, 484–494 for the exchange of notes and the text of the drafts. The United States took the position that if the proposed treaty were to be applicable to Lake Michigan it should be applicable not only to the International Section of the St. Lawrence River but also to the Canadian section above the 45th parallel. See Department of State file 711.42131/74 (National Archives).

25. 61 Stat. 4069.

but rather a unilateral interpretation of its provisions to permit some desired action. Notwithstanding this fact, it remains as part of the international law between the United States and Canada.

Despite its age and shortcomings, the agreement offers a lesson that should not be forgotten. The rapidity with which the provisions of the agreement became technically obsolete illustrates the difficulties involved in drafting an arms-limitation agreement. Indeed the history of the agreement illustrates the fundamental fact that the spirit behind such an agreement is of far greater significance than the language of the treaty.

8

The Role of International Law

Throughout the past century and a half, the optimum utilization of the resources of the Great Lakes has been facilitated by systematic resort to and application of the principles and practices of international law. This use of international law has had an important part in the establishment of the international regime for the Great Lakes that has benefited the citizens of both countries. It has prevented acrimonious international debate over the proper utilization of the resources of the lakes. Rights have been created, generally on a national-treatment basis, that have enabled the citizens of both countries to share to the fullest extent their common inheritance.

The extent to which the rules of international law have been applied in a particular situation has varied with the situation. In some instances there has been merely an application of the customary principles and practices of international law. In other situations the enunciation of new principles of international law (generally in the context of a treaty) proved to be necessary to regulate a particular matter. In a few instances binding rules incorporated into municipal legislation without any formal bilateral agreement have been sufficient for the task. Notwithstanding the variation in the type of international law resorted to (whether conventional rules or customary rules), major problems of the Great Lakes have been alleviated, if not resolved, by the application of the rules and principles of international law as well as by the procedures recognized by the law of nations.

For the establishment of the international boundary through the lakes, the problem was one of definition and delineation. As set forth in the various treaties, the boundary passes through the middle of the lakes (excluding Lake Michigan) and water communications. Generally this was interpreted to mean a median line equidistant from the shores of the lakes, and the boundary was drawn in accordance with that interpretation. In the connecting waterways and rivers, however, where navigation was limited to narrow channels, the principle of the *Thalweg* was adopted—thus ensuring a right of navigation to both parties. The actual delineation of the boundary was accomplished by special international commissions established for that purpose. The final delineation of the boundary was completed in this century by the International Waterways Commission, with the delineation of a straight line boundary on modern charts.

Rules of customary international law were adopted and applied with regard to criminal and admiralty jurisdiction on the lakes. With respect to the former, the rule that a state has jurisdiction over matters within its territory has, of course, been applied to the lakes since they are national waters. In addition courts in both countries have declared that the Great Lakes, because of their size and navigability, may be characterized (for the purpose of criminal jurisdiction) as high seas. Consequently the rule of customary international law that the flag state may exercise jurisdiction over offenses occurring upon its vessels applies to Canadian and American vessels navigating the Great Lakes, even though the vessels may be within the jurisdiction of the other state. In the area of criminal jurisdiction, there is thus a concurrency of jurisdiction; either the flag state or the territorial sovereign may exercise jurisdiction over an offense on the lakes.

In addition to this application of the rules of international law, the old common law rule that admiralty jurisdiction applied only to those inland waters affected by the ebb and flow of the tide was modified by the municipal courts to permit the exercise of admiralty jurisdiction on the Great Lakes. Although the lakes are non-tidal, the courts of both countries have held that admiralty jurisdiction is applicable to them since they are public waters that are navigable in fact. As a consequence the corpus of admiralty law with its amalgam of international and common law is valid as applied to the lakes.

With respect to the rights of navigation, conventional rules predominate. Beginning with the Jay Treaty (1794), the treaty right of free and open navigation of the lakes and connecting waters was gradually extended in various treaties until the citizens of both countries obtained a national-treatment right to navigate freely all portions of the lakes, connecting waters, and canals for the purpose of trade and commerce. It is to be noted that notwithstanding the right of free and open navigation of the lakes for the purpose of trade and commerce, there is no right of free and open navigation for the purpose of commercial fishing. American citizens have obtained a perpetual right to the free and open navigation of the St. Lawrence River from the international boundary to the ocean. Complementary with this right of free and open navigation of the lakes and water communications, uniform and reciprocal practices to facilitate navigation have been adopted. These practices may be found in such matters as the rules of the road, salvage rights, pilotage requirements for ocean-going vessels, quarantine inspection, load line regulations, and communication installations for safety purposes.

In the use and control of the water resources of the lakes, the governments have carefully enunciated in the Boundary Waters Treaty, 1909, the general principles which are to govern this matter. Although this law is conventional law, the rules are compatible with the general principles of international law that require that unilateral riparian utilization of common waters be accomplished without injury to the rights of the co-riparian. During the past half-century, the International Joint Commission has contributed to the successful working of the international regime and the optimum utilization of the water resources by its objective application of the principles specified in the 1909 treaty. Differences have arisen concerning the riparian use of tributary waters (waters which are not actually a part of the international boundary), but both governments have indicated that although such waters are wholly within the jurisdiction of one riparian state, their use will be in accordance with the general principles of international law.

The international law of the Great Lakes relative to naval arms limitation is modest and is associated with controversy. The basic Rush-Bagot Agreement (1817) became technically obsolete within a few decades after its signature; thereafter it was frequently interpreted unilaterally to permit some desired action (generally by the United States to the annoyance of the Canadian government). Despite the violations of the specific provisions, the agreement is still regarded as being in force, although the present-day observance is certainly of the spirit rather than of the letter of the agreement. Prior to and during World War II, several bilateral interpretations were made which helped to bring it up to date.

The international regime has been of least effect in fishery regulation. This is due primarily to the fact that the American fishery is within the jurisdiction of the eight riparian states with the federal government as yet unable to perfect an agreement which would permit it to exercise control over the problem. The present international regime is very limited, consisting primarily of an international commission for the control and eradication of the parasitic sea lamprey and the restoration of certain food fish. Although it may alleviate the present problem of destruction by the sea lamprey, the long-range problem of the gradual depletion of the food fish will certainly require a more ambitious international regime. Whether one with enlarged powers will be established depends, not on the international considerations, but on the domestic problem of obtaining agreement among the eight American states as to the nature and scope of such a regime.

The brief review of the accomplishments of the international regime suggests that the governments' approach to the regime and the problems of the Great Lakes has been pragmatic and realistic. Rules of international law and practice have been adopted and applied because of their contribution to the well-being of the citizens of both countries. The pertinent conventional rules have been the result of negotiation and mutual concession. The unsuccessful American appeal to natural law for support of its claim of a right to navigate the Canadian section of the St. Lawrence River in the 1820's appears to be the only departure from a thoroughly pragmatic approach to the problems of the Great Lakes.

This survey of the international law of the Great Lakes supports the conclusion that the greater portion of the law consists of conventional rules. This is not surprising since the physical facts of the lakes are unique and require laws that are tailored to these facts. Consequently there are treaty provisions governing the rights of navigation, the use and control of the waters, the preservation of the fishery, the definition and delineation of the international boundary, the scope of salvage rights, and the use of radiotelephone installations on vessels for safety purposes. Notwithstanding this preponderance of conventional law, general principles of international law have also been applied to the Great Lakes. This is particularly the case with regard to the exercise of criminal and admiralty jurisdiction on the lakes. Most of these principles have been declared to be applicable to the lakes by the municipal courts. Reciprocal legislation has been effective in some matters. This is especially true with regard to navigation practices such as the rules of the road and pilotage requirements.

It is also clear from this study that there are lacunae in the legal regime for the Great Lakes. These lacunae can best be resolved by the two governments' giving serious consideration to a new treaty similar to the 1932 Deep Waterway Treaty. In addition to its provisions for the construction of the seaway, that treaty also contained important provisions relating to navigation and water usage. In this regard the parties need to set a fixed limit on the amount of water that will be diverted at Chicago, and to prohibit any future diversion into another watershed without the approval of the International Joint Commission. The unperfected 1932 treaty contained appropriate provisions for both matters. In addition provision for compensation for water diverted into the system by one riparian for benefit of the other needs to be set forth. It is also time for the parties to make the navigation of the entire system—including Lake Michigan, the connecting canals, and the Canadian canals in the St. Lawrence—a permanent right. Moreover, there needs to be clear agreement that in time of peace neither party will block the seaway to the vessels of a third state calling at the ports of the other party. With the exception of the last mentioned point and the provision for compensation for diversions into the system, the above items were incorporated into the 1932 treaty and in a proposed draft treaty prepared in 1938. It is now time to conclude the efforts commenced three decades ago.[1]

Although the immediate and primary beneficiaries of the international regime have been the riparian governments and their citizens, it would not be presumptuous to say that the effect of the regime has extended beyond the North American continent. The conventional rules relative to such matters as the use and control of the waters and the rights of free and open navigation have certainly contributed to the progressive development of international law on these subjects. With respect to the former, the incorporation of provisions in the 1909 Boundary Waters Treaty, which establish the principle of the recognition of the rights and interests of both riparians, has helped to advance a principle originally offered *de lege ferenda* to a principle that may now be described correctly as *lex lata*. In connection with the latter, the free and open navigation of the lakes and their connecting waters is another illustration of successful international co-operation.

The effectiveness of the international regime of the Great Lakes is due in part to the intention of the participants to make it work. Even more fundamental, however, is the sense of community which makes for mutual understanding and respect and a disposition to resort to law to resolve differences. James T. Shotwell has described that sense of community as follows:

. . . the North Atlantic triangle presents the supreme example of that which so bewilders the continental mind, Anglo-Saxon policy. No definition can be framed in logical terms which will wholly describe that subtle but unyielding sense of reality within it which dictates conduct according to fundamental rules of equity and fair play. The heritage of freedom is impatient of restraints, but it makes for peace

1. See Great Lakes–St. Lawrence Deep Waterway Treaty, *For. Rel.* (1932), II, 69–78; William R. Willoughby, *The St. Lawrence Waterway* (Madison: University of Wisconsin Press, 1961), pp. 160 ff.; and Canada, *Correspondence and Documents Relating to the Great Lakes–St. Lawrence Basin Development, 1938–1941* (1941).

when it recognizes the similar heritage of others. While these ideals have been departed from on many occasions, and bullying and force have by no means been absent from the history of those who share in the great tradition of democracy, nevertheless there has grown up in nations which share the heritage of freedom a sense that resort to violence is an indecent thing and unthinkable between neighbors, and that, while there is and can be no slacking in defense against aggression, the control of international affairs should be attuned to those ethical principles, which each country works out in its own domestic affairs.[2]

Certainly the international regime is more effective because of the common heritage shared by the participants. It in turn contributes to that heritage and to mutual understanding.

2. James T. Shotwell in his Introduction to John Bartlet Brebner, *North Atlantic Triangle* (New York: Columbia University Press, 1945), p. viii.

Definitive Treaty of Peace, September 3, 1783.

8 *Stat.* 80

Article II

. . . from thence, by a line due west on said latitude [forty-fifth], until it strikes the river Iroquois or Cataraquy [St. Lawrence]; thence along the middle of said river into Lake Ontario, through the middle of said lake until it strikes the communication by water between that lake and Lake Erie; thence along the middle of said communication into Lake Erie, through the middle of said lake until it arrives at the water communication between that lake and Lake Huron; thence along the middle of said water communication into the Lake Huron; thence through the middle of said lake to the water communication between that lake and Lake Superior; thence through Lake Superior northward of the Isles Royal and Phelipeaux, to the Long Lake; thence through the middle of said Long Lake, and the water communication between it and the Lake of the Woods, to the said Lake of the Woods. . . .

Treaty of Washington, May 8, 1871.

18 *Stat.* 335.

Article XXVI

The navigation of the river St. Lawrence, ascending and descending, from the forty-fifth parallel of north latitude, where it ceases to form the boundary between the two countries, from, to, and into the sea, shall forever remain free and open for the purposes of commerce to the citizens of the United States, subject to any laws and regulations of Great Britain, or of the Dominion of Canada, not inconsistent with such privilege of free navigation.

The navigation of the rivers Yukon, Porcupine, and Stikine, ascending and descending, from, to, and into the sea, shall forever remain free and open for the purposes of commerce to the subjects of Her Britannic Majesty and to the citizens of the United States, subject to any laws and regulations of either country within its own territory, not inconsistent with such privilege of free navigation.

The Canadian International Boundary, April 11, 1908.

35 *Stat.* 2003.

Article IV

The High Contracting Parties agree that the existing International Waterways Commission, constituted by concurrent action of the United States and the Dominion of Canada and composed of three Commissioners on the part of the United States and three Commissioners on the part of the Dominion of Canada, is hereby authorized and empowered to ascertain and reestablish accurately the location of the international boundary line beginning at the point of its intersection with the St. Lawrence River near the forty-fifth parallel of north latitude, as determined under Articles I and VI of the Treaty of August 9, 1842, between the United States and Great Britain, and thence through the Great Lakes and communicating waterways to the mouth of the Pigeon River, at the western shore of Lake Superior, in accordance with the description of such line in Article II of the Treaty of Peace between the United States and Great Britain, dated September 3, 1783, and of a portion of such line in Article II of the Treaty of August 9, 1842, aforesaid, and as described in the joint report dated June 18, 1822, of the Commissioners appointed under Article VI of the Treaty of December 24, 1814, between the United States and Great Britain, with respect to a portion of said line and as marked on charts prepared by them and filed with said report, and with respect to the remaining portion of said line as marked on the charts adopted as treaty charts of the boundary under the provisions of Article II of the Treaty of 1842, above mentioned, with such deviation from said line, however, as may be required on account of the cession by Great Britain to the United States of the portion of Horse Shoe Reef in the Niagara River necessary for the light-house erected there by the United States in accordance with the terms of the protocol of a conference held at the British Foreign Office December 9, 1850, between the representatives of the two Governments and signed by them agreeing upon such cession; and it is agreed that wherever the boundary is shown on said charts by a curved line along the water the Commissioners are authorized in their discretion to adopt, in place of such curved line, a series of connecting straight lines defined by distances and courses and following generally the course of such curved line, but conforming strictly to the description of the boundary in the existing treaty provisions, and the geographical coordinates of the turning points of such line shall be stated by said Commissioners so as to conform to the system of latitude and longitudes of the charts mentioned below, and the said Commissioners shall so far as practicable mark the course of the entire boundary line located and defined as aforesaid, by buoys and monuments in the waterways and by permanent range marks established on the adjacent shores or islands, and by such other boundary marks and at such points as in the judgment of the Commissioners it is desirable that the boundary should be so marked; and the line of the boundary defined and located as aforesaid shall be laid down by said Commissioners on accurate modern charts prepared or adopted by them for that purpose, in quadruplicate sets, certified and signed by the Commissioners, two duplicate originals of which shall be filed by them with each Government; and the Commissioners shall also prepare in duplicate and file with each Government a joint report or reports describing in detail the course of said line and the range marks and buoys marking it, and the character and location of each boundary mark. The majority of the Commissioners shall have power to render a decision.

The line so defined and laid down shall be taken and deemed to be the international boundary as defined and established by treaty provisions and the proceedings thereunder as aforesaid from its intersection with the St. Lawrence River to the mouth of Pigeon River.

Reciprocal Rights in the Matters of Conveyance of Prisoners and Wrecking and Salvage, May 18, 1908.

35 *Stat.* 2035.

Article II

The High Contracting Parties agree that vessels and wrecking appliances, either from the United States or the Dominion of Canada, may salve any property wrecked and may render aid and assistance to any vessels wrecked, disabled or in distress in the waters or on the shores of the other country in that portion of the St. Lawrence River through which the International Boundary line extends, and, in Lake Ontario, Lake Erie, Lake St. Clair, Lake Huron, and Lake Superior, and in the Rivers Niagara, Detroit, St. Clair, and Ste Marie, and in the Canals at Sault Ste Marie, and on the shores and in the waters of the other country along the Atlantic and Pacific Coasts within a distance of thirty miles from the International Boundary on such Coasts.

It is further agreed that such reciprocal wrecking and salvage privileges shall include all necessary towing incident thereto, and that nothing in the Customs, Coasting or other laws or regulations of either country shall restrict in any manner the salving operations of such vessels or wrecking appliances.

Vessels from either country employed in salving in the waters of the other shall, as soon as practicable afterwards, make full report at the nearest custom house of the country in whose waters such salving takes place.

Boundary Waters Treaty, January 11, 1909.

36 *Stat.* 2448.

Preliminary Article

For the purposes of this treaty boundary waters are defined as the waters from main shore to main shore of the lakes and rivers and connecting waterways, or the portions thereof, along which the international boundary between the United States and the Dominion of Canada passes, including all bays, arms, and inlets thereof, but not including tributary waters which in their natural channels would flow into such lakes, rivers, and waterways, or waters flowing from such lakes, rivers, and waterways, or the waters of rivers flowing across the boundary.

Article I

The High Contracting Parties agree that the navigation of all navigable boundary waters shall forever continue free and open for the purposes of commerce to the inhabitants and to the ships, vessels, and boats of both countries equally, subject, however, to any laws and regulations of either country, within its own territory, and not inconsistent with such privilege of free navigation and applying equally and without discrimination to the inhabitants, ships, vessels, and boats of both countries.

It is further agreed that so long as this treaty shall remain in force, this same right of navigation shall extend to the waters of Lake Michigan and to all canals connecting boundary waters, and now existing or which may hereafter be constructed on either side of the line. Either of the High Contracting Parties may adopt rules and regulations governing the use of such canals within its own territory and may charge tolls for the use thereof, but all such rules and regulations and all tolls charged shall apply alike to the subjects or citizens of the High Contracting Parties and the ships, vessels, and boats of both of the High Contracting Parties, and they shall be placed on terms of equality in the use thereof.

Article II

Each of the High Contracting Parties reserves to itself or to the several State Governments on the one side and the Dominion or Provincial Governments on the other as the case may be, subject to any treaty provisions now existing with respect thereto, the exclusive jurisdiction and control over the use and diversion, whether temporary or permanent, of all waters on its own side of the line which in their natural channels would flow across the boundary or into boundary waters; but it is agreed that any interference with or diversion from their natural channels of such waters on either side of the boundary, resulting in any injury on the other side of the boundary, shall give rise to the same rights and entitle the injured parties to the same legal remedies as if such injury took place in the country where such diversion or interference occurs; but this provision shall not apply to cases already existing or to cases expressly covered by special agreement between the parties hereto.

It is understood, however, that neither of the High Contracting Parties intends by the foregoing provision to surrender any right, which it may have, to object to any interference with or diversions of waters on the other side of the boundary the effect of which would be productive of material injury to the navigation interests on its own side of the boundary.

Article III

It is agreed that, in addition to the uses, obstructions, and diversions heretofore permitted or hereafter provided for by special agreement between the Parties hereto, no further or other uses or obstructions or diversions, whether temporary or permanent, of boundary waters on either side of the line, affecting the natural level or flow of boundary waters on the other side of the line, shall be made except by authority of the United States or the Dominion of Canada within their respective jurisdictions and with the approval, as hereinafter provided, of a joint commission, to be known as the International Joint Commission.

The foregoing provisions are not intended to limit or interfere with the existing rights of the Government of the United States on the one side and the Government of the Dominion of Canada on the other, to undertake and carry on governmental works in boundary waters for the deepening of channels, the construction of breakwaters, the improvement of harbours, and other governmental works for the benefit of commerce and navigation, provided that such works are wholly on its own side of the line and do not materially affect the level or flow of the boundary waters on the other, nor are such provisions intended to interfere with the ordinary use of such waters for domestic and sanitary purposes.

Article IV

The High Contracting Parties agree that, except in cases provided for by special agreement between them, they will not permit the construction or maintenance on their respective sides of the boundary of any remedial or protective works or any dams or other obstructions in waters flowing from boundary waters or in waters at a lower level than the boundary in rivers, flowing across the boundary, the effect of which is to raise the natural level of waters on the other side of the boundary unless the construction or maintenance thereof is approved by the aforesaid International Joint Commission.

It is further agreed that the waters herein defined as boundary waters and waters flowing across the boundary shall not be polluted on either side to the injury of health or property on the other.

Article V

The High Contracting Parties agree that it is expedient to limit the diversion of waters from the Niagara River so that the level of Lake Erie and the flow of the stream shall not be appreciably affected. It is the desire of both Parties to accomplish this object with the least possible injury to investments which have already been made in the construction of power plants on the United States side of the river under grants of authority from the State of New York, and on the Canadian side of the river under licenses authorized by the Dominion of Canada and the Province of Ontario.

So long as this treaty shall remain in force, no diversion of the waters of the Niagara River above the Falls from the natural course and stream thereof shall be permitted except for the purposes and to the extent hereinafter provided.

The United States may authorize and permit the diversion within the State of New York of the waters of said river above the Falls of Niagara, for power purposes, not exceeding in the aggregate a daily diversion at the rate of twenty thousand cubic feet of water per second.

The United Kingdom, by the Dominion of Canada, or the Province of Ontario, may authorize and permit the diversion within the Province of Ontario of the waters of said river above the Falls of Niagara, for power purposes, not exceeding in the aggregate a daily diversion at the rate of thirty-six thousand cubic feet of water per second.

The prohibitions of this article shall not apply to the diversion of water for sanitary or domestic purposes, or for the service of canals for the purpose of navigation.

Article VII

The High Contracting Parties agree to establish and maintain an International Joint Commission of the United States and Canada composed of six commissioners, three on the part of the United States appointed by the President thereof, and three on the part of the United Kingdom appointed by His Majesty on the recommendation of the Governor in Council of the Dominion of Canada.

Article VIII

This International Joint Commission shall have jurisdiction over and shall pass upon all cases involving the use or obstruction or diversion of the waters with respect to which under Articles III and IV of this Treaty the approval of this Commission is required, and in passing upon such cases the Commission shall be governed by the following rules or principles which are adopted by the High Contracting Parties for this purpose:

The High Contracting Parties shall have, each on its own side of the boundary, equal and similar rights in the use of the waters hereinbefore defined as boundary waters.

The following order of precedence shall be observed among the various uses enumerated hereinafter for these waters, and no use shall be permitted which tends materially to conflict with or restrain any other use which is given preference over it in this order of precedence:

(1) Uses for domestic and sanitary purposes;
(2) Uses for navigation, including the service of canals for the purposes of navigation;
(3) Uses for power and for irrigation purposes.

The foregoing provisions shall not apply to or disturb any existing uses of boundary waters on either side of the boundary.

The requirement for an equal division may in the discretion of the Commission be suspended in cases of temporary diversions along boundary waters at points where such equal division can not be made advantageously on account of local conditions, and where such diversion does not diminish elsewhere the amount available for use on the other side.

The Commission in its discretion may make its approval in any case conditional upon the construction of remedial or protective works to compensate so far as possible for the particular use or diversion proposed, and in such cases may require that suitable and adequate provision, approved by the Commission, be made for the protection and indemnity against injury of any interests on either side of the boundary.

In cases involving the elevation of the natural level of waters on either side of the line as a result of the construction or maintenance on the other side of remedial or protective works or dams or other obstructions in boundary waters or in waters flowing therefrom or in waters below the boundary in rivers flowing across the boundary, the Commission shall require, as a condition of its approval thereof, that suitable and adequate provision, approved by it, be made for the protection and indemnity of all interests on the other side of the line which may be injured thereby.

The majority of the Commissioners shall have power to render a decision. In case the Commission is evenly divided upon any question or matter presented to it for decision, separate reports shall be made by the Commissioners on each side to their own Government. The High Contracting Parties shall thereupon endeavour to agree upon an adjustment of the question or matter of difference and if an agreement is reached between them, it shall be reduced to writing in the form of a protocol, and shall be communicated to the Commissioners, who shall take such further proceedings as may be necessary to carry out such agreement.

Article IX

The High Contracting Parties further agree that any other questions or matters of difference arising between them involving the rights, obligations, or interests of either in relation to the other or to the inhabitants of the other, along the common frontier between the United States and the Dominion of Canada, shall be referred from time to time to the International Joint Commission for examination and report, whenever either the Government of the United States or the Government of the Dominion of Canada shall request that such questions or matters of difference be so referred.

The International Joint Commission is authorized in each case so referred to examine into and report upon the facts and circumstances of the particular questions and matters referred, together with such conclusions and recommendations as may be appropriate, subject, however, to any restrictions or exceptions which may be imposed with respect thereto by the terms of the reference.

Such reports of the Commission shall not be regarded as decisions of the questions or matters of difference so submitted either on the facts or the law, and shall in no way have the character of an arbitral award.

The Commission shall make a joint report to both Governments in all cases in which all or a majority of the Commissioners agree, and in case of disagreement the minority may make a joint report to both Governments, or separate reports to their respective Governments.

In case the Commission is evenly divided upon any question or matter referred to it for report, separate reports shall be made by the Commissioners on each side to their own Government.

Article X

Any questions or matters of difference arising between the High Contracting Parties involving the rights, obligations, or interests of the United States or of the Dominion of Canada either in relation to each other or to their respective inhabitants, may be referred for decision to the International Joint Commission by the consent of the two Parties, it being understood that on the part of the United States any such action will be by and with the advice and consent of the Senate, and on the part of His Majesty's Government with the consent of the Governor General in Council. In each case so referred, the said Commission is authorized to examine into and report upon the facts and circumstances of the particular questions and matters referred, together with such conclusions and recommendations as may be appropriate, subject, however, to any restrictions or exceptions which may be imposed with respect thereto by the terms of the reference.

A majority of the said Commission shall have power to render a decision or finding upon any of the questions or matters so referred.

If the said Commission is equally divided or otherwise unable to render a decision or finding as to any questions or matters so referred, it shall be the duty of the Commissioners to make a joint report to both Governments, or separate reports to their respective Governments, showing the different conclusions arrived at with regard to the matters or questions so referred for decision by the High Contracting Parties to an umpire chosen in accordance with the procedure prescribed in the fourth, fifth, and sixth paragraphs of Article XLV of the Hague Convention for the pacific settlement of international disputes, dated October 18, 1907. Such umpire shall have power to render a final decision with respect to those matters and questions so referred on which the Commission failed to agree.

Niagara River Treaty, February 27, 1950.

1 U.S.T. 694.

Article II

The United States of America and Canada agree to complete in accordance with the objectives envisaged in the final report submitted to the United States of America and Canada on December 11, 1929, by the Special International Niagara Board, the remedial works which are necessary to enhance the beauty of the Falls by distributing the waters so as to produce an unbroken crestline on the Falls. The United States of America and Canada shall request the International Joint Commission to make recommendations as to the nature and design of such remedial works and the allocation of the task of construction as between the United States of America and Canada. Upon approval by the United States of America and Canada of such recommendations the construction shall be undertaken pursuant thereto under the supervision of the International Joint Commission and shall be completed within four years after the date upon which the United States of America and Canada shall have approved the said recommendations. The total cost of the works shall be divided equally between the United States of America and Canada.

Article III

The amount of water which shall be available for the purposes included in Articles IV and V of this Treaty shall be the total outflow from Lake Erie to the Welland Canal and the Niagara River (including the Black Rock Canal) less the amount of water used and necessary for domestic and sanitary purposes and for the service of canals for the purpose of navigation. Waters which are being diverted into the natural drainage of the Great Lakes System through the existing Long Lac-Ogoki works shall continue to be governed by the notes exchanged between the Government of the United States of America and the Government of Canada at Washington on October 14 and 31 and November 7, 1940, and shall not be included in the waters allocated under the provisions of this Treaty.

Article IV

In order to reserve sufficient amounts of water in the Niagara River for scenic purposes, no diversions of the water specified in Article III of this Treaty shall be made for power purposes which will reduce the flow over Niagara Falls to less than one hundred thousand cubic feet per second each day between the hours of eight A.M., E.S.T., and ten P.M., E.S.T., during the period of each year beginning April 1 and ending September 15, both dates inclusive, or to less than one hundred thousand cubic feet per second each day between the hours of eight A.M., E.S.T., and eight P.M., E.S.T., during the period of each year beginning September 16 and ending October 31, both dates inclusive, or to less than fifty thousand cubic feet per second at any other time; the minimum rate of fifty thousand cubic feet per second to be increased when additional water is required for flushing ice above the Falls or through the rapids below the Falls. No diversion of the amounts of water, specified in this Article to flow over the Falls, shall be made for power purposes between the Falls and Lake Ontario.

Article V

All water specified in Article III of this Treaty in excess of water reserved for scenic purposes in Article IV may be diverted for power purposes.

Article VI

The waters made available for power purposes by the provisions of this Treaty shall be divided equally between the United States of America and Canada.

•   •   •   •   •

Article VIII

Until such time as there are facilities in the territory of one party to use its full share of the diversions of water for power purposes agreed upon in this Treaty, the other party may use the portion of that share for the use of which facilities are not available.

Article IX

Neither party shall be responsible for physical injury or damage to persons or property in the territory of the other which may be caused by any act authorized or provided for by this Treaty.

Great Lakes Fisheries, September 10, 1954.

6 U.S.T. 2836.

Article I

This Convention shall apply to Lake Ontario (including the St. Lawrence River from Lake Ontario to the forty-fifth parallel of latitude), Lake Erie, Lake Huron (including Lake St. Clair), Lake Michigan, Lake Superior and their connecting waters, hereinafter referred to as "the Convention Area." This Convention shall also apply to the tributaries of each of the above waters to the extent necessary to investigate any stock of fish of common concern, the taking or habitat of which is confined predominantly to the Convention Area, and to eradicate or minimize the population of the sea lamprey (*Petromyzon marinus*) in the Convention Area.

Article II

1. The Contracting Parties agree to establish and maintain a joint commission, to be known as the Great Lakes Fishery Commission, hereinafter referred to as "the Commission," and to be composed of two national sections, a Canadian Section and a United States Section. Each Section shall be composed of not more than three members appointed by the respective Contracting Parties.

2. Each Section shall have one vote. A decision or recommendation of the Commission shall be made only with the approval of both Sections.

3. Each Contracting Party may establish for its Section an advisory committee for each of the Great Lakes. The members of each advisory committee so established shall have the right to attend all sessions of the Commission except those which the Commission decides to hold *in camera*.

. . . . .

Article IV

The Commission shall have the following duties:

(a) to formulate a research program or programs designed to determine the need for measures to make possible the maximum sustained productivity of any stock of fish in the Convention Area which, in the opinion of the Commission, is of common concern to the fisheries of the United States of America and Canada and to determine what measures are best adapted for such purpose;

(b) to coordinate research made pursuant to such programs and, if necessary, to undertake such research itself;

(c) to recommend appropriate measures to the Contracting Parties on the basis of the findings of such research programs;

(d) to formulate and implement a comprehensive program for the purpose of eradicating or minimizing the sea lamprey populations in the Convention Area; and

(e) to publish or authorize the publication of scientific and other information obtained by the Commission in the performance of its duties.

Article V

In order to carry out the duties set forth in Article IV, the Commission may:

(a) conduct investigations;

(b) take measures and install devices in the Convention Area and the tributaries thereof for lamprey control; and

(c) hold public hearings in the United States of America and Canada.

. . . . .

Article X

Nothing in this Convention shall be construed as preventing any of the States of the United States of America bordering on the Great Lakes or, subject to their constitutional arrangements, Canada or the Province of Ontario from making or enforcing laws or regulations within their respective jurisdictions relative to the fisheries of the Great Lakes so far as such laws or regulations do not preclude the carrying out of the Commission's duties.

Article XI

The Contracting Parties agree to enact such legislation as may be necessary to give effect to the provisions of this Convention.

Great Lakes—St. Lawrence Deep Waterway Treaty, July 18, 1932.

(unperfected)

For Rel., 1932, II, 69–75.

Article VII

The High Contracting Parties agree that the rights of navigation accorded under the provisions of existing treaties between the United States of America and His Majesty shall be maintained, notwithstanding the provisions for termination contained in any of such treaties, and declare that these treaties confer upon the citizens or subjects and upon the ships, vessels and boats of each High Contracting Party, rights of navigation in the St. Lawrence River, and the Great Lakes System, including the canals now existing or which may hereafter be constructed.

Article VIII

The High Contracting Parties, recognizing their common interest in the preservation of the levels of the Great Lakes System, agree:

(a) 1. that the diversion of water from the Great Lakes System, through the Chicago Drainage Canal, shall be reduced by December 31st, 1938, to the quantity permitted as of that date by the decree of the Supreme Court of the United States of April 21st, 1930;

2. in the event of the Government of the United States proposing, in order to meet an emergency, an increase in the permitted diversion of water and in the event that the Government of Canada takes exception to the proposed increase, the matter shall be submitted, for final decision, to an arbitral tribunal which shall be empowered to authorize, for such

time and to such extent as is necessary to meet such emergency, an increase in the diversion of water beyond the limits set forth in the preceding sub-paragraph and to stipulate such compensatory provisions as it may deem just and equitable; the arbitral tribunal shall consist of three members, one to be appointed by each of the Governments, and the third, who will be the Chairman, to be selected by the Governments;

(b) that no diversion of water, other than the diversion referred to in paragraph (a) of this Article, from the Great Lakes System or from the International Section to another watershed shall hereafter be made except by authorization of the International Joint Commission;

(c) that each Government in its own territory shall measure the quantities of water which may at any point be diverted from or added to the Great Lakes System, and shall place the said measurements on record with the other Government semi-annually;

(d) that, in the event of diversions being made into the Great Lakes System from watersheds lying wholly within the borders of either country, the exclusive rights to the use of waters equivalent in quantity to any waters so diverted shall, notwithstanding the provisions of Article IV(a), be vested in the country diverting such waters, and the quantity of water so diverted shall be at all times available to that country for use for power below the point of diversion, so long as it constitutes a part of boundary waters;

(e) that compensation works in the Niagara and St. Clair Rivers, designed to restore and maintain the lake levels to their natural range, shall be undertaken at the cost of the United States as regards compensation for the diversion through the Chicago Drainage Canal, and at the cost of Canada as regards the diversion for power purposes, other than power used in the operation of the Welland Canals; the compensation works shall be subject to adjustment and alteration from time to time as may be necessary, and as may be mutually agreed upon by the Governments, to meet any changes effected in accordance with the provisions of this Article in the water supply of the Great Lakes System above the said works, and the cost of such adjustment and alteration shall be borne by the Party effecting such change in water supply.

Dockets of the International Joint Commission Relating to the Great Lakes—St. Lawrence

Docket number	Year	Title
4	1912	Pollution of Boundary Waters
5	1912	Livingstone Channel
6, 8	1913	Michigan Northern Power Company and Algoma Steel Corporation, Limited
13	1916	St. Clair River Channel
14	1918	New York and Ontario Power Company
15	1918	St. Lawrence River Power Company
17	1920	St. Lawrence River Navigation and Power Investigation
21	1925	Buffalo and Fort Erie Public Bridge Company
24	1928	St. Lawrence River Power Company
54	1946	Pollution of Boundary Waters—St. Clair River, Lake St. Clair, Detroit River, St. Mary's River
55	1948	Pollution of Boundary Waters—Niagara River
61	1949	Air Pollution Detroit—Windsor Area
62	1950	Niagara Falls
67	1952	Lake Ontario Levels
68	1952	St. Lawrence Power Project
74	1961	Niagara Reference (2d)
75	1961	Niagara Application
78	1963	Niagara Falls
79	1964	Lake Erie—Niagara River Ice Boom Application
82	1964	Great Lakes Levels

Selected Bibliography

Public Documents

American State Papers, Foreign Relations.
Annotated Indiana Statutes (Burns, 1956).
British and Foreign State Papers.
Canada. *Naval Vessels on the Great Lakes, Correspondence, 1892–1917.* Ottawa, n.d.
———. *Report of the Royal Commission on Coasting Trade, 1957.* Ottawa: Queen's Printer, 1958.
———. *Statutes at Large.*
———. *Statutory Orders and Regulations, Consolidation, 1955.* 3 vols.
Canada, Archives. *Documents Relating to the Constitutional History of Canada, 1819–1828.* Ottawa: Patenaude, 1935.
Canada, Department of External Affairs. *Correspondence Relating to International Boundary Waters.* 3 vols. Ottawa: n.d.
———. *Treaties and Agreements Affecting Canada in Force Between His Majesty and the United States of America, 1814–1913.* Ottawa: King's Printer, 1915.
Canada, House of Commons, Standing Committee on Marine and Fisheries. *Minutes of Proceedings and Evidence.* No. 1, 1955.
Canada, House of Commons, Standing Committee on Railways, Canals and Telegraph Lines. *Minutes of Proceedings and Evidence.* No. 6, 1961.
Canada, Parliament. "Complied Reports of the International Waterways Commission, 1905–1913," *Sessional Papers,* No. 19a, XLVII, No. 12, 1913.
———. "Correspondence or Papers with the Colonial Office, or with the Government of the United States, in Regard to the Action of that Government in Denying the Free Navigation of the United States Canals, in Accordance with the Washington Treaty," *Sessional Papers,* No. 111, IX, No. 8, 1876.
———. "Lake Grain Rates Report," *Sessional Papers,* No. 211, LIX, No. 6, 1923.

———. "Messages, Despatches, and Minutes of the Privy Council, Relating to the Treaty of Washington," *Sessional Papers,* No. 18, V, No. 6, 1872.

———. "Papers Relating to the Chicago Drainage Canal," *Sessional Papers,* No. 180, LX, No. 7, 1924.

———. "Papers Relating to the St. Lawrence Waterway Project," *Sessional Papers,* No. 101 c,d,e,f, 157, LX, No. 7, 1924.

The Canada Gazette, Statutory Orders and Regulations.

The Canadian Abridgment.

Compiled Laws of the State of Michigan (1948).

Congressional Record.

Consolidated Laws of New York, Annotated.

Department of State Bulletin.

Dominion Marine Association. "Submission of Dominion Marine Association to Minister of Transport for Canada in Matter of Government Assistance to the Canadian Shipping Industry." Toronto, 1961. (Mimeographed.)

———. "Submission of Dominion Marine Association to Royal Commission on Coasting Trade of Canada." Toronto, 1955. (Mimeographed.)

Federal Register.

Final Report of the International Joint Commission on the Pollution of Boundary Waters Reference. Washington: Government Printing Office, 1918.

Great Britain. *Statutes at Large.*

Great Lakes and Central Region, Bureau of Commercial Fishery. *Commercial Fisheries Development: A Long Range Program.* Ann Arbor, 1960.

Great Lakes Commission. *Great Lakes Foreign Commerce, 1958.* Ann Arbor, n.d.

———. *Great Lakes Port Organization and Administration.* Ann Arbor, n.d.

Great Lakes Fishery Commission. *Annual Report.*

Hackworth, Green H. *Digest of International Law.* 8 vols. Washington: Government Printing Office, 1940–1944.

Illinois Annotated Statutes (Smith-Hurd).

International Board of Inquiry for the Great Lakes Fisheries. *Report and Supplement.* Washington: Government Printing Office, 1943.

International Joint Commission. *In the Matter of the Application of the St. Lawrence River Power Company.* Ottawa: King's Printer, 1919.

———. *Michigan Northern Power Company and Algoma Steel Corporation, Applications, Proceedings.* Washington: Government Printing Office, 1917.

————. *Pollution of Boundary Waters Reference, Proceedings*. Washington: Government Printing Office, 1917.

————. *Report of the International Joint Commission on the Pollution of Boundary Waters*. 1950.

————. *Report of the International Joint Commission on the Pollution of the Atmosphere in the Detroit River Area*. Washington, 1960.

————. *Rules of Procedure and Text of Treaty*. Washington: Government Printing Office, 1947.

————. *Safeguarding Boundary Water Quality*. 1961.

International Waterways Commission. *Report of the International Waterways Commission upon the International Boundary between the Dominion of Canada and the United States through the St. Lawrence River and Great Lakes*. Ottawa: Government Printing Bureau, 1916.

League of Nations Treaty Series.

Malloy, William M., comp. *Treaties, Conventions, International Acts, Protocols and Agreements between the United States of America and Other Powers, 1776–1909*. 2 vols. Washington: Government Printing Office, 1910.

Mason's Michigan Supplement (1956).

Miller, David Hunter, ed. *Treaties and Other International Acts of the United States of America*. 8 vols. Washington: Government Printing Office, 1931–1948.

Minnesota Statutes Annotated.

Moore, John Bassett. *A Digest of International Law*. 8 vols. Washington: Government Printing Office, 1906.

————. *History and Digest of the International Arbitrations to Which the United States Has Been a Party*. 6 vols. Washington: Government Printing Office, 1898.

Official Opinions of the Attorney General of the United States.

Official Report of the Debates of the House of Commons of the Dominion of Canada.

Ohio Revised Code Annotated (Page).

Papers Relating to the Foreign Relations of the United States.

Plumb, Ralph G. *History of the Navigation of the Great Lakes*. Washington: Government Printing Office, 1911.

Purdon's Pennsylvania Statutes Annotated.

Report of Fred K. Nielsen, American and British Claims Arbitration. Washington: Government Printing Office, 1926.

The Revised Statutes of Canada.

St. Lawrence Waterway, Report of the Joint Board of Engineers Appointed by the Government of the United States and Canada on the Improvement of the St. Lawrence River between Lake

Ontario and Montreal and on Related Questions Referred to the Board by the Two Governments. Washington: Government Printing Office, 1927.

Treaties and Other International Acts Series.

U. N. Economic Commission for Europe, Committee on Electric Power. *Legal Aspects of the Hydro-Electric Development of Rivers and Lakes of Common Interest.* E/ECE/136. Geneva, 1952.

United States. *Statutes at Large.*

U. S. Army, Corps of Engineers. *Effect on Great Lakes and St. Lawrence River of an Increase of 1000 Cubic Feet per Second in the Diversion at Chicago.* 1957.

———. *Great Lakes Pilot, 1959.* Detroit: U. S. Lake Survey, 1959.

———. *Waterborne Commerce of the United States, 1959.* Part 3, Great Lakes.

U. S. Coast Guard. *Rules of the Road: Great Lakes.* Washington: Government Printing Office, 1959.

U. S. Department of Commerce. *Navigation Laws of the United States, 1940.* Washington: Government Printing Office, 1940.

———. *The St. Lawrence Survey.* 7 Parts. Washington: Government Printing Office, 1940.

U. S. Department of Commerce, Maritime Administration. *Domestic Oceanborne and Great Lakes Commerce of the United States, 1955–1958.* Washington: Government Printing Office, 1960.

———. *The Handbook of Merchant Shipping Statistics Through 1958.* Washington: Government Printing Office, n.d.

U. S. Department of State. *Northern Boundary of the United States.* Washington: Government Printing Office, 1906.

———. *Treaties in Force: A List of Treaties and Other International Agreements of the United States in Force on January 1, 1965.* Washington: Government Printing Office, n.d.

U. S. House of Representatives. *Amending Section 272 of the Penal Code.* Report No. 1163. 61st Cong., 2d Sess., 1910.

———. *Boundary between the United States and Great Britain.* Executive Document No. 451. 25th Cong., 2d Sess., 1838.

———. *Free Navigation of the St. Lawrence.* Report No. 295. 31st Cong., 1st Sess., 1850.

———. *Granting the Consent of Congress to a Great Lakes Basin Compact.* Report No. 2587. 85th Cong., 2d Sess., 1958.

———. *Lake Levels, Report of the Special Master Charles E. Hughes to the Supreme Court of the United States.* Document 178. 70th Cong., 1st Sess., 1928.

———. *Navigation on the Great Lakes.* Report No. 1682. 52d Cong., 3d Sess., 1895.

————. *Preservation of the Fisheries in Waters Contiguous to the United States and Canada.* Document No. 315. 54th Cong., 2d Sess., 1897.

————. *Protection and Preservation of Food Fishes in International Boundary Waters of the United States and Canada.* Document No. 638. 61st Cong., 2d Sess., 1910.

————. *Providing for Certain Pilotage Requirements in the Navigation of U. S. Waters of the Great Lakes.* Report No. 1666. 86th Cong., 2d Sess., 1960.

————. *Reciprocal Trade with Canada.* Executive Document No. 64. 31st Cong., 1st Sess., 1850.

————. *Report of the Second Meeting of the Canada–United States Interparliamentary Group.* Report No. 730. 86th Cong., 1st Sess., 1959.

————. *Requiring a Study to Be Conducted of the Effect of Increasing the Diversion of Water from Lake Michigan into the Illinois Waterway for Navigation, and for Other Purposes.* Report No. 191. 86th Cong., 1st Sess., 1959.

————. *Safety on the Great Lakes by Means of Radio.* Report No. 2284. 83d Cong., 2d Sess., 1954.

————. *Trade with the British Provinces.* Executive Document No. 240. 40th Cong., 2d Sess., 1868.

————. *Transporting Iron Ore on the Great Lakes by Canadian Vessels.* Report No. 1713. 79th Cong., 2d Sess., 1946.

————. *War Vessels on the Great Lakes.* Document 471. 56th Cong., 1st Sess., 1900.

U. S. House of Representatives, Committee on Foreign Affairs. *Hearings on the Great Lakes Basin Compact.* 85th Cong., 2d Sess., 1958.

U. S. House of Representatives, Committee on Merchant Marine and Fisheries. *Hearings on Minimum Age at Sea Convention, 1936.* 76th Cong., 3d Sess., 1940.

U. S. House of Representatives, Committee on Public Works. *Lake Michigan Water Diversion.* 86th Cong., 1st Sess., 1959.

U. S. House of Representatives, Committee on Rivers and Harbors. *Hearings on Illinois and Mississippi Rivers, and Diversion of Water from Lake Michigan.* 67th Cong., 2d Sess., 1922.

————. *Hearings on Illinois River, and the Abstraction of Water from Lake Michigan.* 69th Cong., 1st Sess., 1926.

————. *Hearings on the Illinois Waterway—Diversion of Water from Lake Michigan.* 78th Cong., 1st Sess., 1943.

————. *Illinois and Mississippi Rivers, and Diversion of Water from Lake Michigan.* 68th Cong., 1st Sess., 1924.

U. S. Senate. *Amending Title 46, United States Code, Section 251.* Report No. 2364. 81st Cong., 2d Sess., 1950.

————. *Canada–United States Interparliamentary Group.* Document No. 27. 87th Cong., 1st Sess., 1961.

————. *Convention with Canada for the Development, Protection, and Conservation of the Fisheries of the Great Lakes.* Executive C. 79th Cong., 2d Sess., 1946.

————. *Diversion of Water from Lake Michigan at Chicago.* Report No. 808. 86th Cong., 1st Sess., 1959.

————. *Final Report of the International Waterways Commission upon the Proposed Dam at the Outlet of Lake Erie.* Document No. 118. 63d Cong., 1st Sess., 1913.

————. *Granting the Consent of Congress to a Great Lakes Basin Compact.* Report No. 1888. 85th Cong., 2d Sess., 1958.

————. *Granting the Consent of Congress to a Great Lakes Basin Compact.* Report No. 231. 86th Cong., 1st Sess., 1959.

————. *Great Lakes Fisheries Convention.* Executive Report No. 7. 84th Cong., 1st Sess., 1955.

————. *International Convention for the Prevention of Pollution of Sea by Oil.* Executive C. 86th Cong., 2d Sess., 1960.

————. *International Labor Organization Convention.* Executive L. 86th Cong., 2d Sess., 1960.

————. *Legal Aspects of the Use of Systems of International Waters.* Document No. 118. 85th Cong., 2d Sess., 1958.

————. *Naval Forces on the Great Lakes.* Executive Document No. 9, 52d Cong., 2d Sess., 1892.

————. *Officers' Competency Certificates Convention, 1936.* Report No. 677. 76th Cong., 1st Sess., 1939.

————. *Pilotage Requirements, for Vessels Navigating the U. S. Waters of the Great Lakes.* Report No. 1284. 86th Cong., 2d Sess., 1960.

————. *Preservation and Improvement of the Scenic Beauty of the Niagara Falls and Rapids.* Document No. 128. 71st Cong., 2d Sess., 1930.

————. *Reciprocal Trade with Canada.* Executive Document 114. 52d Cong., 1st Sess., 1892.

————. *Report of Israel D. Andrews on the Trade and Commerce of the British North American Colonies.* Executive Document No. 112. 32d Cong., 1st Sess., 1853.

————. *Report of the Secretary of Treasury on Trade with British American Colonies.* Executive Document No. 23. 31st Cong., 2d Sess., 1851.

————. *St. Lawrence Seaway Manual.* Document No. 165. 83d Cong., 2d Sess., 1955.

———. *St. Lawrence Waterway.* Document No. 114. 67th Cong., 2d Sess., 1922.

———. *St. Lawrence Waterway.* Document No. 179. 67th Cong., 2d Sess., 1922.

———. *St. Lawrence Waterway Project.* Document No. 183. 69th Cong., 2d Sess., 1927.

U. S. Senate, Committee on Foreign Relations. *Hearings and Proceedings on Treaty between United States and Canada Concerning Boundary Waters.* 61st Cong., 2d Sess., 1910.

———. *Hearings on Columbia River Treaty.* 87th Cong., 1st Sess., 1961.

———. *Hearings on International Convention for the Prevention of Pollution of the Seas by Oil.* 86th Cong., 2d Sess., 1960.

———. *Hearings on Water Treaty with Mexico.* 79th Cong., 1st Sess., 1945.

U. S. Senate, Committee on Interior and Insular Affairs and a Special Subcommittee of the Committee on Foreign Relations. *Joint Hearings on Upper Columbia River Development.* 84th Cong., 2d Sess., 1956.

U. S. Senate, Merchant Marine and Fisheries Subcommittee of the Committee of Interstate and Foreign Commerce. *Hearings on Great Lakes Pilotage.* 86th Cong., 2d Sess., 1960.

U. S. Senate, Subcommittee of Committee on Foreign Relations. *Hearings on Great Lakes Basin Compact.* 84th Cong., 2d Sess., 1956.

———. *Hearings on Great Lakes Fisheries Convention.* 84th Cong., 1st Sess., 1955.

———. *Hearings on St. Lawrence Waterway.* 72d Cong., 2d Sess., 1932.

U. S. Senate, Subcommittee of the Committee on the Judiciary. *Hearings on Great Lakes Basin Compact.* 85th Cong., 2d Sess., 1958.

U. S. Senate, Subcommittee on Flood Control and Rivers and Harbors of the Committee on Public Works, and the Committee on Public Works of the House of Representatives. *Joint Hearings on Niagara Power Development.* 83d Cong., 1st Sess., 1953.

U. S. Senate, Subcommittee on Merchant Marine and Fisheries of the Committee on Commerce. *Hearings on the Economic Impact of Low Water Levels in the Great Lakes.* 88th Cong., 2d Sess., 1964.

U. S. Senate, Subcommittee on Public Works. *Hearings on Diversion of Water from Lake Michigan.* 85th Cong., 2d Sess., 1958.

———. *Hearings on Lake Michigan Water Diversion.* 83d Cong., 2d Sess., 1954.

———. *Hearings on Lake Michigan Water Diversions.* 84th Cong., 2d Sess., 1956.

———. *Hearings on Water Diversion from Lake Michigan.* 86th Cong., 1st Sess., 1959.

Wharton, Francis, ed. *The Revolutionary Diplomatic Correspondence of the United States.* 6 vols. Washington: Government Printing Office, 1889.

Whiteman, Marjorie M. *Digest of International Law.* 4 vols. Washington: Government Printing Office, 1964.

Wisconsin Statutes (1957).

Witmer, T. Richard, ed. *Documents on the Use and Control of the Waters of Interstate and International Streams.* Washington: Government Printing Office, 1956.

Books

Adami, Colonnello Vittorio. *National Frontiers in Relation to International Law.* Translated by T. T. Behrens. London: Oxford University Press, 1927.

American Bar Association, Section of International and Comparative Law. *Proceedings, 1959.*

Barrett, George F. *The Waterway from the Great Lakes to the Gulf of Mexico.* Chicago: The Sanitary District of Chicago, 1926.

Baxter, Richard R. *The Law of International Waterways.* Cambridge, Mass.: Harvard University Press, 1964.

Bemis, Samuel Flagg. *The Diplomacy of the American Revolution.* New York: D. Appleton-Century, 1935.

———. *Jay's Treaty: A Study in Commerce and Diplomacy.* New York: Macmillan, 1923.

Berber, F. J. *Rivers in International Law.* New York: Oceana Publications, 1959.

Bindoff, S. T. *The Scheldt Question to 1839.* London: Allen and Unwin, 1945.

Bloomfield, L. M., and Fitzgerald, G. F. *Boundary Waters Problems of Canada and the United States.* Toronto: Carswell, 1958.

Boggs, S. Whittemore. *International Boundaries: A Study of Boundary Functions and Problems.* New York: Columbia University Press, 1940.

Borden, Henry, ed. *Robert Laird Borden: His Memoirs.* 2 vols. New York: Macmillan, 1938.

Brebner, J. Bartlet. *Canada.* Ann Arbor: University of Michigan Press, 1960.

———. *North Atlantic Triangle.* New York: Columbia University Press, 1945.

Briggs, Herbert W., ed. *The Law of Nations.* 2nd ed. New York: Appleton-Century-Crofts, 1952.

Burt, A. L. *The United States, Great Britain, and British North America.* New Haven: Yale University Press, 1940.

Callahan, James Morton. *American Foreign Policy in Canadian Relations.* New York: Macmillan, 1937.

———. *The Neutrality of the American Lakes and Anglo-American Relations.* Johns Hopkins Studies in Historical and Political Science Series, XVI. Baltimore, 1898.

Chacko, Chirakaikaran Joseph. *The International Joint Commission between the United States of America and the Dominion of Canada.* New York: Columbia University Press, 1932.

Channing, Edward, and Lansing, Marion Florence. *The Story of the Great Lakes.* New York: Macmillan, 1909.

Colombos, C. John. *The International Law of the Sea.* 4th ed. revised. London: Longmans, 1959.

Cooley, Lyman E. *The Diversion of the Waters of the Great Lakes by Way of the Sanitary and Ship Canal of Chicago.* Chicago: Board of Trustees of the Sanitary District, 1913.

Cooper, John C. *The Right to Fly.* New York: Holt, 1947.

Corbett, P. E. *The Settlement of Canadian-American Disputes.* New Haven: Yale University Press, 1937.

Corey, Albert B. *Canadian-American Relations along the Detroit River.* Detroit: Wayne State University Press, 1957.

Creighton, D. C. *The Commercial Empire of the St. Lawrence, 1760–1850.* Toronto: Ryerson Press, 1937.

Cushing, Caleb. *The Treaty of Washington.* New York: Harper, 1893.

Dawson, R. MacGregor. *William Lyon Mackenzie King: A Political Biography, 1874–1923.* Vol. I. Toronto: University of Toronto Press, 1958.

Deener, David R., ed. *Canada–United States Treaty Relations.* Durham, N. C.: Duke University Press, 1963.

———. *The United States Attorneys General and International Law.* The Hague: Martinus Nijhoff, 1957.

Delafield, Major Joseph. *The Unfortified Boundary.* Edited with an introduction and notes by Robert McElroy and Thomas Riggs. New York: Privately Printed, 1943.

Doughty, Sir Arthur G. *The Elgin-Grey Papers, 1846–1852.* 4 vols. Ottawa: Patenaude, 1937.

Falconer, Sir Robert. *The United States as a Neighbour.* Cambridge: Cambridge University Press, 1926.

Gadizikowski, Gilbert R. *Impact on the Economy of Michigan of Proposed Additional Diversion of Lake Michigan Water at Chicago.* Kalamazoo: W. E. Upjohn Institute for Employment Research, 1963.

Gilmore, Grant, and Charles L. Black, Jr. *The Law of Admiralty.* Brooklyn: Foundation Press, 1957.

Glazebrook, G. P. deT. *Canadian External Relations: An Historical Study to 1914.* New York: Oxford University Press, 1942.

————. *A History of Transportation in Canada.* Toronto: Ryerson Press, 1938.

Grotius, Hugo. *De Jure Belli ac Pacis Libre Tres.* Translated by Francis W. Kelsey. Oxford: Clarendon Press, 1925.

Hartley, Joseph R. *The Effect of the St. Lawrence Seaway on Grain Movements.* Bloomington: Indiana University School of Business, Bureau of Business Research, 1957.

Harvey, A. B., ed. *Tremeear's Annotated Criminal Code.* 5th ed. Calgary: Borroughs, 1944.

Hatcher, Harlan. *The Great Lakes.* London: Oxford University Press, 1944.

Havighurst, Walter. *The Long Ships Passing.* New York: Macmillan, 1942.

Healey, James C. *Foc's'le and Glory-Hole.* New York: Merchant Marine Publishers Association, 1936.

Hertslet's Commercial Treaties. Vol. III.

Hill, Charles E. *Leading American Treaties.* New York: Macmillan, 1922.

Hill, Norman. *Claims to Territory in International Law and Relations.* London: Oxford University Press, 1945.

Hills, T. L. *The St. Lawrence Seaway.* New York: Praeger, 1959.

Hodge, William. *Papers Concerning Early Navigation on the Great Lakes.* Buffalo: Bigelow Bros., 1883.

Hohman, Elmo Paul. *History of American Merchant Seamen.* Hamden, Conn.: The Shoe String Press, 1956.

Hooker, Nancy Harvison, ed. *The Moffat Papers.* Cambridge: Harvard University Press, 1956.

Howard, Sister Jane Mary. *Some Economic Aspects of the St. Lawrence Project.* Washington, D. C.: Catholic University of America Press, 1949.

Howe, Walter A., comp. *Documentary History of the Illinois and Michigan Canal.* Illinois Division of Waterways, 1956.

Hutchinson, Bruce. *The Struggle for the Border.* New York: Longmans, 1955.

Hyde, Charles Cheney. *International Law Chiefly as Interpreted and Applied by the United States.* 3 vols. 2d ed. revised. Boston: Little, Brown Co., 1945.

L'Institut de Droit International. *Annuaire.* Vols. XXIV, XLVIII.

International Law Association. *Report of the Forty-Seventh Conference, Dubrovnik, 1956.*

———. *Report of the Forty-Eighth Conference, New York, 1958.*
Ireland, Tom. *The Great Lakes—St. Lawrence Deep Waterway to the Sea.* New York: Putnam, 1934.
Jessup, Philip C. *Elihu Root.* 2 vols. New York: Dodd, Mead and Co., 1938.
———. *The Law of Territorial Waters and Maritime Jurisdiction.* New York: G. A. Jennings, 1927.
Johnston, Henry P., ed. *The Correspondence and Public Papers of John Jay.* 4 vols. New York: Putnam, 1890–1893.
Jones, Stephen B. *Boundary-Making: A Handbook for Statesmen, Treaty Editors and Boundary Commissioners.* Washington: Carnegie Endowment for International Peace, 1945.
Kaeckenbeeck, G. *International Rivers.* London: Grotius Society, 1918.
Keenleyside, Hugh L., and G. S. Brown. *Canada and the United States.* Rev. ed. New York: Knopf, 1952.
Knauth, Arnold W. *Knauth's Benedict on Admiralty.* 7th ed. Vols. VI, VIa. New York: Baker, Voorhis, 1958.
Kyte, George W. *Organization and Work of the International Joint Commission.* Ottawa: Patenaude, 1937.
Lauterpacht, H. *The Function of Law in the International Community.* Oxford: Clarendon Press, 1933.
Leonard, L. Larry. *International Regulation of Fisheries.* Washington: Carnegie Endowment for International Peace, 1944.
Levermore, Charles H. *The Anglo-American Agreement of 1817.* World Peace Foundation Pamphlet Series, Vol. IV, No. 4, 1914.
Limitation of Armament on the Great Lakes. Carnegie Endowment for International Peace, Division of International Law, Pamphlet No. 2, 1914.
McClure, Wallace. *International Executive Agreements.* New York: Columbia University Press, 1941.
McInnis, Edgar W. *The Unguarded Frontier.* New York: Doubleday, Doran, 1942.
Mackenzie, Norman, and Laing, Lionel H. *Canada and the Law of Nations.* Toronto: Ryerson Press, 1938.
Manning, William R. *Diplomatic Correspondence of the United States: Canadian Relations, 1784–1860.* 4 vols. Washington: Carnegie Endowment for International Peace, 1940–1943.
Moore, Charles, ed. and comp. *The St. Mary's Falls Canal.* Detroit: The Semi-Centennial Commission, 1907.
Moore, David R. *Canada and the United States, 1815–1830.* Chicago: Press of Jennings & Graham, 1910.
Moulton, Harold G., Morgan, Charles S., and Lee, Adah L. *The St. Lawrence Navigation and Power Project.* Washington, D. C.: Brookings Institution, 1929.

Ogilvie, Paul Morgan. *International Waterways.* New York: Macmillan, 1920.

Pickersgill, J. W. *The Mackenzie King Record, 1939–1944.* Vol. I. Toronto: University of Toronto Press, 1960.

Pope, Joseph. *Memoirs of the Right Honourable Sir John Alexander Macdonald.* 2 vols. Ottawa: Durie and Son, n.d.

Reiff, Henry. *The United States and the Treaty Law of the Sea.* Minneapolis: University of Minnesota Press, 1959.

St. Lawrence Seaway and Power Project. Montreal: Reid and Boulton, 1958.

Savelle, Max. *The Diplomatic History of the Canadian Boundary, 1749–1763.* New Haven: Yale University Press, 1940.

Schuyler, Eugene. *American Diplomacy and the Furtherance of Commerce.* New York: Charles Scribner, 1886.

Scott, F. R. *Canada and the United States.* Boston: World Peace Foundation, 1941.

Shippee, Lester Burrell. *Canadian American Relations, 1849–1874.* New Haven: Yale University Press, 1939.

Skelton, Oscar Douglas. *Life and Letters of Sir Wilfrid Laurier.* 2 vols. New York: Century, 1922.

Smith, Goldwin. *The Treaty of Washington, 1871.* Ithaca: Cornell University Press, 1941.

Smith, Herbert Arthur. *The Economic Uses of International Rivers.* London: P. S. King, 1931.

——, ed. *Great Britain and the Law of Nations.* 2 vols. London: P. S. King, 1932–1935.

Stacey, C. P. *The Undefended Border: The Myth and the Reality.* Ottawa: Canadian Historical Association Booklets, 1953.

Stephens, George Washington. *The St. Lawrence Waterway Project.* Montreal: Louis Carrier, 1930.

Stewart, Robert B. *Treaty Relations of the British Commonwealth of Nations.* New York: Macmillan, 1939.

Tansill, Charles Callan. *Canadian-American Relations, 1875–1911.* New Haven: Yale University Press, 1943.

——. *The Canadian Reciprocity Treaty of 1854.* Baltimore: Johns Hopkins Press, 1922.

Vattel, E. de. *The Law of Nations.* Translated by Charles Fenwick. Washington: Carnegie Institution, 1916.

Water Pollution and the Great Lakes. Proceedings of a Conference held May 15, 16, 1961 by De Paul University, Chicago, Illinois.

Willoughby, William R. *The St. Lawrence Waterway.* Madison: University of Wisconsin Press, 1961.

Wilson, Robert R. *The International Law Standard in Treaties of the United States.* Cambridge, Mass.: Harvard University Press, 1953.

————. *United States Commercial Treaties and International Law.* New Orleans: Hauser Press, 1960.

Wright, C. P. *The St. Lawrence Deep Waterway: A Canadian Appraisal.* Toronto: Macmillan, 1935.

Articles

Adams, Milton P. "Water Pollution Control in the Great Lakes Region," *University of Detroit Law Journal,* XXXVII (1959–1960), 96–120.

Adams, Paul L. "Diversion of Lake Michigan Waters," *University of Detroit Law Journal,* XXXVII (1959–1960), 149–156.

Anderson, Chandler P. "The St. Lawrence Waterway Project," *American Journal of International Law,* XXVI (1932), 110–113.

"Approval of Recommendations for Controlling Levels of Lake Ontario," *Department of State Bulletin,* XXXIV (1956), 89–92.

Austin, Jacob. "Canadian–United States Practice and Theory Respecting the International Law of International Rivers: A Study of the History and Influence of the Harmon Doctrine," *The Canadian Bar Review,* XXXVII (1959), 393–443.

Bacon, Ruth E. "British and American Policy and the Right of Fluvial Navigation," *British Yearbook of International Law,* XIII (1932), 76–92.

Baxter, Richard R. "Passage of Ships through International Waterways in Time of War," *British Yearbook of International Law,* XXXI (1954), 187–216.

Bedard, Charles M. "Les Relations canado-americaines et le regime juridique des Grand Lacs," *Culture,* XIV (1953), 111–142.

Borchard, Edwin. "The St. Lawrence Waterway and Power Project," *American Journal of International Law,* XLIII (1949), 411–434.

"Boundaries on Great Lakes—Accretion and Reliction—Effect of Meander Line," *Michigan Law Review,* XXVI (1927–1928), 906–916.

Bourne, C. B. "The Columbia River Controversy," *The Canadian Bar Review,* XXXVII (1959), 444–472.

Brown, George W. "The Opening of the St. Lawrence to American Shipping," *Canadian Historical Review,* VII (1926), 4–12.

————. "The St. Lawrence Waterway in the Nineteenth Century," *Queen's Quarterly,* XXXV (1928), 628–642.

Burchell, Charles J. "Canadian Admiralty Jurisdiction and Shipping Laws," *The Law Quarterly Review,* XLV (1929), 370–377.

Burpee, Lawrence J. "From Sea to Sea," *Canadian Geographical Journal,* XVI (1938), 3–32.

————. "The International Joint Commission," *Journal of the Society of Comparative Legislation,* XVI (new series) (1916), 5–12.

Callahan, J. M. "Agreement of 1817—Reduction of Naval Forces upon the American Lakes," *Annual Report of the American Historical Association,* 1895, pp. 367–392.

———. "Northern Lake Frontier during Civil War," *Annual Report of the American Historical Association,* 1896, pp. 355–359.

"The Canadian-American Partnership," *Department of State Bulletin,* XXIX (1953), 735–738.

Carman, Ernest C. "Sovereign Rights and Relations in the Control and Use of American Waters," *Southern California Law Review,* III (1929–1930), 84–100, 152–172, 266–319.

Clute, William K. "The Title to Alluvial Lands along the Michigan Shores of the Great Lakes as Affected by the Indefeasible Trust Doctrine Applicable to State Ownership of Lake Bottom," *Michigan State Bar Journal,* IX (1929–1930), 199–221.

Cohen, Maxwell, and Nadeau, Gilbert. "The Legal Framework of the St. Lawrence Seaway," in Paul O. Proehl, ed., *Legal Problems of International Trade.* Urbana: University of Illinois Press, 1959, pp. 29–50.

Colson, Frederick D. "Title to Beds of Lakes in New York," *The Cornell Law Quarterly,* IX (1923–1924), 288–317.

"Complaints concerning High Water Levels in Lake Ontario," *Department of State Bulletin,* XXVI (1952), 903.

Dealey, J. Q., Jr. "The Chicago Drainage Canal and the St. Lawrence Development," *American Journal of International Law,* XXIII (1929), 307–328.

Eagleton, Clyde. "The Use of Waters of International Rivers," *The Canadian Bar Review,* XXXIII (1955), 1018–1034.

Eayrs, James. "A 'Low and Dishonest Decade': Aspects of Canadian External Policy, 1931–1939," in Hugh L. Keenleyside *et al., The Growth of Canadian Policies in External Affairs.* Durham, N. C.: Duke University Press, 1960, pp. 59–80.

Garner, J. W. "The Chicago Sanitary District Case," *American Journal of International Law,* XXII (1928), 837–840.

Gibbons, Alan O. "Sir George Gibbons and the Boundary Waters Treaty of 1909," *Canadian Historical Review,* XXXIV (1953), 124–138.

Goldie, D. M. M. "Effect of Existing Uses on the Equitable Apportionment of International Rivers: A Canadian View," *University of British Columbia Law Review,* I (1960), 399–408.

Griffin, William L. "A History of the Canadian–United States Boundary Waters Treaty of 1909," *University of Detroit Law Journal,* XXXVII (1959–1960), 76–95.

———. "The Use of Waters of International Drainage Basins under

Customary International Law," *American Journal of International Law*, LIII (1959), 50–80.

Gutteridge, H. C. "Abuse of Rights," *Cambridge Law Journal*, V (1933), 22–45.

Harrison, Kenneth S., and Byrd, John H., Jr. "A Survey of United States Jurisdiction over Foreign Vessels," *Federal Bar Journal*, XIX (1959), 152–161.

Higgins, Elmer. "Fish Outlive Officials," *State Government*, XI (1938), 53–54, 58.

Hile, Ralph. "Fishing Regulations," *The Fisherman*, XX (1952), 5, 12, 14.

Hoagland, Henry Elmer. "Wage Bargaining on the Vessels of the Great Lakes," *University of Illinois Studies in the Social Sciences*, VI, No. 3 (1917).

Hunt, Harry E. "How the Great Lakes Became 'High Seas' and Their Status Viewed from the Standpoint of International Law," *American Journal of International Law*, IV (1910), 285–313.

Hutchins, Wells A., and Steele, Harry A. "Basic Water Rights Doctrines and Their Implications for River Basin Development," *Law and Contemporary Problems*, XXII (1957), 276–300.

Hyde, Charles Cheney. "Notes on Rivers and Navigation in International Law," *American Journal of International Law*, IV (1910), 145–155.

"The International Joint Commission between the United States and Canada," *American Journal of International Law*, VI (1912), 191–197.

Jessup, Philip C. "The Great Lakes—St. Lawrence Deep Waterway Treaty," *American Journal of International Law*, XXVI (1932), 814–819.

Jimenez de Arechaga, Eduardo. "International Legal Rules Governing Use of Waters from International Watercourses," *Inter-American Law Review*, II (1960), 329–339.

Johnson, Ralph W. "The Columbia River System," in American Society of International Law, *Proceedings* (1960), pp. 120–134.

———. "Effect of Existing Uses on the Equitable Apportionment of International Rivers: An American View," *University of British Columbia Law Review*, I (1960), 389–398.

Kunen, James L. "International Negotiations concerning the St. Lawrence Project," *University of Detroit Law Journal*, XXXIII (1955–1956), 14–36.

La Forest, G. V. "May the Provinces Legislate in Violation of International Law?," *Canadian Bar Review*, XXXIX (1961), 78–92.

Lawford, H. J. "Treaties and Rights of Transit on the St. Lawrence," *Canadian Bar Review*, XXXIX (1961), 577–602.

Lawrence, Henry. "Waterways Problems on the Canadian Boundary," *Foreign Affairs*, IV (1925–1926), 556–573.

Laylin, John G. "Indus River System—Comments," in American Society of International Law, *Proceedings* (1960), pp. 144–150.

———. "Principles of Law Governing the Uses of International Rivers," in American Society of International Law, *Proceedings* (1957), pp. 20–36.

Lynde, Cornelius. "The Controversy Concerning the Diversion of Water from Lake Michigan by the Sanitary District of Chicago," *Illinois Law Review*, XXV (1930), 243–260.

Macdonald, R. St. J. "International Law—Jay Treaty of 1794—Abrogation of Treaties by Outbreak of War—Review of Canadian and Foreign Decisions," *Canadian Bar Review*, XXXIV (1956), 602–612.

MacKay, Robert A. "The International Joint Commission between the United States and Canada," *American Journal of International Law*, XXII (1928), 292–318.

Martin, Charles E. "The Diversion of Columbia River Waters," in American Society of International Law, *Proceedings* (1957), pp. 2–10.

Mayer, Harold M. "The St. Lawrence Seaway and Problems of the Great Lakes States," *State Government*, XXIX (1956), 25–29, 38.

Mills, Dudley A. "British Diplomacy and Canada," *United Empire*, II (new series) (1911), 684–712.

Myers, Denys P. "Contemporary Practice of the United States Relating to International Law," *American Journal of International Law*, LIII (1959), 896–922.

Naujoks, Herbert H. "The Chicago Water Diversion Controversy," *Marquette Law Review*, XXX (1946–1947), 149–176, 228–271.

"Naval Vessels on the Great Lakes," *Department of State Bulletin*, IV (1941), 366–372.

"Navigable Waters—Power of the State to Alienate Land under Waters of the Great Lakes," *Michigan Law Review*, XXVI (1927–1928), 339–340.

"Navigation and Other Uses of International Rivers and Canals," in American Society of International Law, *Proceedings* (1957), pp. 2–56.

Olis, Anthony A., and Sprecher, Robert A. "Legal Aspects of Lake Diversion," *Northwestern University Law Review*, LI (1957), 653–674.

Patton, M. J. "Shipping and Canals," in Adam Shortt and Arthur G.

Doughty, eds., *Canada and Its Provinces.* Vol. X. Toronto: Edinburgh University Press, 1914, pp. 475–626.

Piper, Don C. "Navigation Provisions in United States Commercial Treaties," *American Journal of Comparative Law,* XI (1962), 184–204.

——. "The Role of Intergovernmental Machinery in Canadian-American Relations," *South Atlantic Quarterly,* LXII (1963), 551–574.

——. "A Significant Docket for the International Joint Commission," *American Journal of International Law,* LIX (1965), 593–597.

——. "Two International Waterways Commissions: A Comparative Study," *Virginia Journal of International Law,* VI (1965), 98–112.

"Poor Fish—in the Great Lakes," *State Government,* XI (1938), 51–52.

Potter, William W. "Michigan's Rights in the Waters of the Great Lakes," *Michigan State Bar Journal,* VII (1927–1928), 75–83.

Power, John F. "Littoral Rights on the Great Lakes," *Notre Dame Lawyer,* XX (1944–1945), 424–428.

Scott, Robert D. "The Canadian-American Boundary Waters Treaty: Why Article II?," *The Canadian Bar Review,* XXXVI (1958), 511–547.

Scott, W. B. "The Ownership and Use of Rivers and Streams in the Province of Quebec," *The Canadian Bar Review,* XVII (1939), 221–232.

Selak, Charles B., Jr. "The United States—Canadian Great Lakes Fisheries Convention," *American Journal of International Law,* L (1956), 122–129.

Shotwell, James T. "The International Significance of the Canadian-American Peace Tradition," *Conference on Educational Problems in Canadian-American Relations.* Orono, Maine: University of Maine Press, n.d., pp. 3–12.

Simsarian, James. "The Diversion of Waters Affecting the United States and Canada," *American Journal of International Law,* XXXII (1938), 488–518.

Smith, Durand. "The Great Lakes Fisheries Convention," *Department of State Bulletin,* XVI (1947), 643–644, 675.

Smith, H. A. "The Chicago Diversion," *British Yearbook of International Law,* X (1929), 144–157.

——. "The Chicago Diversion," *The Canadian Bar Review,* VIII (1930), 330–343.

——. "Diversion of International Waters," *British Yearbook of International Law,* XI (1930), 195–196.

Sprague, George C. "The Extension of Admiralty Jurisdiction and the

Growth of Substantive Maritime Law in the United States since 1835," *Law: A Century of Progress, 1835–1935.* Vol. III. New York: New York University Press, 1937, pp. 294–341.

Stern, Robert L. "Legal Problems in the St. Lawrence Seaway Project," in International and Comparative Law Section, American Bar Association, *Proceedings* (1954), pp. 57–69.

Swibold, Gretchen. "The Lake Levels Controversy," *Current Economic Comment,* XXII (1960), 51–61.

Thompson, Joseph B. "Title to Land under Navigable Waters in New York," *Columbia Law Review,* XXI (1921), 680–695.

"U. S., Canada Refer Lake Ontario Complaints to Joint Commission," *Department of State Bulletin,* XXVII (1952), 67.

"U. S.—Canadian Construction of Power Works in St. Lawrence River Authorized," *Department of State Bulletin,* XXVII (1952), 1019–1024.

Vallance, William Roy. "The Settlement of International Boundary Waters Questions in North America," in Inter-American Academy of International and Comparative Law, *Cursos Monógráphicos.* Vol. VII. Havana, 1959, pp. 261–302.

Vanek, D. C. "Is International Law Part of the Law of Canada?," *The University of Toronto Law Journal,* VIII (1949–1950), 251–297.

VanOosten, John. "From Cisco to Perch to Pike," *State Government,* XI (1938), 55–57.

Walton, Ivan H. "Developments on the Great Lakes, 1815–1943," *Michigan History Magazine,* XXVII (1943), 72–142.

Watts, A. D. "The Protection of Alien Seamen," *International and Comparative Law Quarterly,* VII (1958), 691–711.

Weber, Eugene W. "Activities of the International Joint Commission, United States and Canada," *Sewage and Industrial Wastes,* XXXI (1959), 71–77.

Williams, Clifton. "Who Owns the Bed of Lake Michigan?," *Marquette Law Review,* XII (1927), 12–17.

Willmann, Hildegard. "The Chicago Diversions from Lake Michigan," *The Canadian Bar Review,* X (1932), 575–583.

Wilson, Robert R. "The Commonwealth and the Law of Nations," in Nicholas Mansergh *et al., Commonwealth Perspectives.* Durham, N. C.: Duke University Press, 1958, pp. 59–85.

Archival Material

Department of State file (National Archives).

George C. Gibbons papers (Public Archives of Canada).

Governor General file (Public Archives of Canada).
R. L. Borden papers (Public Archives of Canada).
Wilfrid Laurier papers (Public Archives of Canada).

Unpublished Material

Dunlop, C. C. "The Origin and Development of the International Joint
    Commission as a Judicial Tribunal." Unpublished M.A. thesis,
    Queen's University, 1959.

Index